THAT MAKES SENSE

65 Short Tested Business Principles that Work but are Rarely Taught

By Richard K Stanislaw

That Makes Sense

65 Short Tested Business Principles that Work but are Rarely Taught

RICHARD K STANISLAW

DEDICATION

This book is dedicated to my loving wife Janice; my wonderful children Scott, Alinda, Bobbi, Kelly, and Kimberly; their spouses; my spunky grandkids Ellery, Evan, Sarah, Jacob, Matthew, and Tyler, and all the co-workers who through the years experienced the principles prescribed in this book and embraced the results. Their encouragement was inspirational.

TABLE OF CONTENTS

INTRODUCTION

I love comedy acts, and in the past, I would sometimes laugh so much my stomach would hurt. Other times I was just plain disappointed. I often wondered why some comedians were funnier than others. One day the curiosity got the best of me and I decided to analyze it. It took some time to figure it out, but I found two fundamental reasons: 1) their style and 2) funny skits had content that stated the obvious which, for whatever reason, wasn't so obvious to the audience.

For example, comedian Johnny Steele presented a routine on American laziness and fast food restaurants that had drive up windows. His skit was pretending to describe a McDonald's style restaurant to an 8 year old from a third world country, who only knew helping his family grow beans, feed the goats, harvest the crop, slaughter the animals, cook the food, and eat the much labored resulting meal. Johnny said "in America most people don't grow their own food, nor harvest crops, slaughter the animals, or cook it; instead someone does that for us and we just eat the food. Farmers grow the food, ranchers raise the cattle, and truck drivers deliver the food to what we call fast food restaurants located on just about every corner, which owners hire people to prepare the food for us to eat. All we need to do is drive our cars to these locations and retrieve the meals. We don't even need to get out of our cars because the restaurants have these windows you can drive right alongside and someone will bring your chosen food directly to the window. The skit when on and on and I laughed a lot because it was true, we are lazy relative to the third world kids and it was obvious when put in that context, but not so obvious while picking up your food at the drive-up window.

Much in the same manner, the book "That Makes Sense" is a collection of the obvious, but not so obvious principles that can be applied to real life situations. Over the years, I have collected all the material presented in the book based on actual life experiences. I preached these doctrines to my five children, who may accuse me of hounding them, but I doubt will accuse me of not helping them in life. I now wish to share the material not just with my kids, but also with anyone who wishes to improve their chances of success in the world.

Each chapter is a self-contained topic and as you read the book, you may say "That Makes Sense" because it is obvious.

1

Push the Pencil

When Evan was very young and inexperienced, he was asked to participate in due diligence of a potential acquisition. Not knowing what due diligence meant, but not wanting to appear ignorant Evan approached Scott (the experienced leader) and asked him, "What do you want me to do?" Scott replied immediately "inventory," which didn't make Evan feel any better because he still didn't know what to do. Evan summoned courage and asked again, "What do you want me to do in inventory?" Scott again answered without hesitation, but this time with forcefulness, "Push the Pencil."

Evan remained confused, so with great bravery went to Scott again and using equal forcefulness asked, "What does push the pencil mean?"

Scott laughed and said, "I was waiting for you to ask that question and wanted to see how many times you would try to clarify your job assignment. You passed the first test. You kept trying to eliminate the fuzziness," Scott told

Evan, "most people just remain in a foggy state accomplishing very little. I send them back to the office. I am not sending you back yet, but you still need to pass one more test."

The second test, Scott explained, was to push the pencil; a metaphor for just start; get a piece of paper and write down what you would want to know if you were personally buying a Company that had millions of dollars in inventory. Start writing, don't stop and don't worry. Forget any checklist or how-to book you may find. Look at those after you fill up the paper.

Scott was smart; he knew Evan had conviction. After all, Evan had already passed test #1. Scott, however, wanted to see if Evan could demonstrate confidence in his own common sense and avoid being paralyzed by the trappings of more experienced surroundings. Scott explained," half the battle in the business world when things are somewhat fuzzy is just to start," or, as Scott had called it Push the Pencil.

Evan quickly grabbed a sheet of paper and started pushing that pencil (today people would use a tablet, of course). He passed test #2, but more importantly he took a giant step in his career by just pushing that pencil. Evan went on to become a CEO years later and to this day gives Scott credit for much of his success. Evan saved the pencil. He shows it to others when he wants to help them within their careers.

2

Trade Gold for Platinum

How many times have you heard "Do unto others as you would have them do unto yourself"? It's the Golden Rule. It's famous. Your mother probably told you the Golden Rule over and over again. Yet, I'm suggesting not practicing it.

Why? Because people are different, have different desires, and different pain thresholds based on their experiences in life. The automatic assumption that our likes or dislikes are shared by everybody else is simply illogical and to treat others the way we would like to be treated when others do not necessarily want that treatment makes little sense.

Case in point: in some cities in the world, although people are harsh to each other in their day-to-day dealings, if you watch them closely you will see that, they don't seem to take offense. They are accustomed to this approach when dealing with people and they subconsciously know it does not offend. However, take these same people and put them in a city where polite conversation is expected and they don't do very well. Sure, they practice the golden rule. They treat people in the same manner they would like to be been treated, but displease regardless, because these people don't prefer that treatment.

A far better approach is to practice the Platinum Rule. "Do unto others as; <u>they</u> would have them do unto <u>themselves</u>." Note that, under this rule, you are forced to find out about other people's likes and dislikes. That is not true with the Golden Rule, where it is assumed that how you like to be treated is how everyone wants to be treated. Under the Platinum Rule you become externalized and more aware of the external factors that shape how others, not you, see the world. Your experience doesn't matter as much.

Granted the exception is running up against someone who is unethical, in which case, common sense needs to come into play. Nonetheless, the next time you hear "go for the gold," remember that the price of platinum is higher than the price of the purest grade of gold.

3

The Ant and the Grasshopper

Rob, the ant, worked hard during the summer months and not only created a nice place to live but also accumulated much-needed food for the winter months soon to arrive. Rob was ready for the harshness of winter.

On the other hand, Gary the grasshopper just hopped around during the summer, had a good time, and was totally unprepared for the brutal winter to come.

The winter arrived and Gary the grasshopper had no place to live and was starving. Rob, the ant, felt sorry for Gary and in a compassionate move gave him some leftover food and side shelter so he would not die. Both the food and shelter were not the best, but they kept the grasshopper alive.

Gary was grateful at first, but as time passed the grasshopper started complaining that Rob had a better quality of life. The grasshopper rallied others until someone with the authority stepped in and forced the ant to share his food and shelter equally with the grasshopper.

Rob the ant was not happy about it, and when the next summer came Rob was not as motivated as he was the previous summer. Rob knew he would be forced to share equally with Gary the grasshopper who, once again, worked very little. As a result, Rob did not find the best place to live nor amass as much food.

The winter came again and the quality of living went down for both Rob the ant and Gary the grasshopper. Near the end of the winter, they almost ran out of food and were forced to ration it to survive.

You may ask, "What do an ant and grasshopper have anything to do with business?" Everything, of course; business is no different from ants and grasshoppers living in a world where some work hard and others do not but both reap the same rewards. In a business, if you fail to reward those who achieve more than those who do not, eventually the results will deteriorate across the board. It is as simple as that.

By the way, Rob the ant became even more de-motivated after the second winter and moved to a different location where he would not be penalized. Gary the grasshopper, therefore, invited another lazy grasshopper. Both had fun during the ensuing summer months but when the winter came Gary and the other grasshopper starved and froze to death.

4

Sounds Like An Excuse To Me (SLAETM)

Craig always had a reason for arriving late or not showing up at all. He also seemed to have a skill to rationalize his failure to complete most tasks assigned to him. He often ignored requests from his boss or co-workers hoping their request would be forgotten in due course. Sometimes they forgot and sometimes they did not, but Craig never worried because he knew he could always talk his way out of anything. That is because Craig learned at an early age how to give great excuses. Indeed, Craig became so good at excuses that he deceived anyone who expected results for any task he really didn't want to do.

Over time, the great feelings that Craig received by achieving results was not as high as the feeling he would get using his very likable personality to side-step the expectations of him. Craig began to wonder why work so hard and why worry about it since he was so good at giving excuses. One of his favorite excuses was explaining how he had to spend so much time on other matters. He had many more. Craig also knew that cracking jokes would help people overlook why a task wasn't done. Craig became lazy and after a while did only what he felt like doing, and not what was expected of him.

Unfortunately, there are a lot of Craigs out there and dealing with them is difficult. The trick is to make one huge but often valid assumption; every time a requested job is not done, no matter what a person says, assume it is an excuse. That's right: every single time, no exceptions. Simply say, "SLAETM," an acronym for Sounds Like an Excuse to Me.

Don't worry. You're not being harsh. If a person committed to complete a task, then it should have been completed. Otherwise, the commitment should not have been made in the first place. Failing to recognize this simple truth is failing to hold individuals accountable. It's nice to feel empathy for some employees, especially if they have been working very hard, but being nice doesn't help them in the long run and it certainly doesn't get results. You're just encouraging bad habits. Sure, there may have been a hurricane or the building burnt down, maybe something like a death in the family, but short of that, it's only an excuse: "SLAETEM."

Pay little attention to the reasons Craig may give. He may say you asked him to do another task and he focused on the latest request. He may say he has been working hard and couldn't quite get it done. Whatever reason he gives, it's a moot point. Your immediate reply should always be "SLAETM."

Remember, Craig should have a list of all open items and every new request should be assessed with those items in mind. Any re-prioritizing should be made at the time of the request. Silence is automatic confirmation that it can be done in a timely manner. Craig is not given a pass of a previous request just because a new request came in. Craig is required to mesh all requests and determine a reasonable promise date. Anything short of that is "SLAETM."

5

I Haven't Been The Same Since That House Fell On My Sister

Did you get out of the wrong side of the bed? Feel like Grumpy in Snow White? That happens, but don't ever consider an excuse. Simply don't go there. It's just a rationalization for your actions that are about to happen or, even worse, already happened.

Far too often mood swings are discussed as if they are OK because an event occurred at home or something went wrong a couple of hours ago, but at work the show must go on. Mood swings are just taboo.

In business, we must learn to keep an even temperament and master this very fast. Here are a few tips:

1. Understand why you feel moody. Analyze what happened that caused the negative change with the intent of stopping it the next time it raises its ugly head.

2. Never rationalize moodiness.

3. View the day from a much higher 50,000 foot level and realize it is not the end of the world.

4. Use an interrupter such as a slap on your leg or a slap on your cheek to remind yourself to calm down.

5. Use a positive trigger that recalls some moment in time that was so uplifting that the associated feelings of just thinking about it reverse the negative.

6. Practice, practice, practice and get through the day flawlessly.

There may be other tricks that work for you. Try them all. Master mood swings. If you do not, they will master you. The next thing you know your face will turn green, you'll favor brooms, and houses will unexplainably fall on your siblings.

6

Ted Made The Biggest Error Of All

Mistakes are made all the time. Ask Jim. He was told by his boss Ted, that all he ever does is make mistakes. "I'm sorry Jim, but there are just too many errors so I'm letting you go," Ted proclaimed. These were the words Jim remembers last hearing before departing the company.

Ted didn't have a problem firing Jim since Jim did, indeed, make many mistakes. It also was easy for Ted to terminate Jim because Ted had lots of practice. Ted had fired just about everybody that had ever worked directly for him. It seems that most of the people who reported directly to Ted also made many mistakes.

Nevertheless, Ted was always surprised to learn that many of the employees he had terminated did very well in their new endeavors especially Jim who advanced to a Vice President. Ted rationalized that they got lucky, but when you dig into it a little deeper, you find that it wasn't luck at all. They were individuals who were high performers except when they worked for Ted.

That's because Ted created fear in making decisions, fear in taking action, and fear in making mistakes. He did this by treating all errors the same regardless of the circumstances.

Ted failed to realize that errors can take many forms but fall only into two categories: 1) errors resulting from action and 2) errors resulting from inaction. The first type of error comes from the heart, from trying to be a team player, to help the cause, and to win. The second type of error comes from complacency, from an "I don't care" attitude, from a "don't expect me to stick my neck out" approach, from "it's not my job" mentality.

If an error occurs as a result of action, the first category, it represents inexperience. That can be corrected through education. It is worth investing time with these people because you're dealing with the up-and-coming high achievers. However, if an error occurs from the second category (errors made from inaction), it represents people who more than likely should not be with the company. It is these people and only these people that should be fired if mistakes are too frequent.

Ted, however, fired people from both categories and without realizing it Ted was eliminating his future success. He was guaranteeing that errors resulting from actions did not occur, but errors from inaction occurred frequently because people feared Ted's punishments.

It is no wonder Ted had so much experience firing people. He failed to understand the fundamental difference in errors.

Eventually, Ted got a new boss. His name was Jacob. Unfortunately for Ted, Jacob understood Ted's management style, despised those who were accustomed to habitually terminating employees for making action errors, and eventually fired Ted.

7

If It Is Worth Doing It Is Worth Doing Imperfectly Only Bo Derek Was A Perfect 10

Some people get things done others don't. It is a simple truth, and while there are many reasons why, one big factor is that results oriented individuals always complete any task 85% first, then after it is up and running go back to finish the less important 15%. They recognize that planning is good but only if it is in proportion to achieving results. It takes time to plan. It takes even more time to plan "perfectly" so that every nook and cranny is determined ahead of time.

Effective people don't initially concern themselves with efficiency. They first and foremost ensure the attainment of planned results; then and only then, do they worry about doing it faster, easier, and more cost-effectively.

The ineffective person believes that somehow efficiency will result in effectiveness. They spend hours upon hours discussing every detail and they tend to lose sight of the original goal. They fall into the trap of believing time doesn't matter. But time does matter. Every goal whether it is to attain an adequate return on investment or install a system to achieve the stated objective; has a time limit. It may not be said officially, but it's there. Time passes and many other issues come into play. The goal currently on the plate may die for lack of importance in today's climate. Those who believe efficiency is as important as the effectiveness simply run out of time.

Efficiency concerns the manner in which the process occurs, but effectiveness is why you're spending any time on the matter in the first place.

An effective person knows that the end result is what's important and ignores those Nay Sayers who practice bashing the process. Nay Sayers could care less about the true end results. They just want to be perfect. But only Bo Derek was a perfect 10.

8

The Truth Can Still Be A Pinocchio

I have five black and white dogs. Three are black. That is an absolutely true statement. Nevertheless, it is still a lie. Why? Because I own four black dogs and one white, not two white dogs as I led you to believe. The statement that I own three black dogs is on its face true, but when true statements attempt to mislead you, to bring you to false conclusions, they are no different than bold-faced lies.

In the business world, this happens all the time. The CEO gives a report to the shareholders about the health of the company. The CEO reveals how the profits last year were excellent again because of the high renewal rates of the top 5 service contracts. However, the CEO fails to disclose that just last week two of the five top service contracts were awarded to the competition. The CEO's statement is on its face the truth, but failing to disclose that two contracts were lost misleads the shareholders into believing the future will be the same as the past when in reality there is now a real challenge to find replacement orders.

The CEO may have conveyed the truth, but nevertheless it is a lie. The CEO told a half-truth.

Keep in mind these half-truths as I call them are usually created in order to be judged in a favorable light. The dog owner wanted the recipient to believe he had two white dogs for some reason or he would have said I own 5 black and white dogs 4 are black. The CEO wanted people to believe the company is OK and will be fine in the future. Both were misleading statements. Both were half-truths. Both were lies.

This type of behavior needs to be checked. Simply ask the commenter to confirm what you are concluding. Mr. Dog owner does that mean you have two white dogs? Ms. CEO, do you expect the 5 top service contracts to continue?

Pinocchio's nose grew whenever he told a straight-out lie, but most humans don't directly lie; instead they fib by omission through a half-truth. Indeed, if noses really grew because of half-truths, humans would look more like elephants.

9

Numbers Are Not Politicians

Numbers are not affiliated with a political party and are not beholding to anyone or anything. Therefore, they make the best answers to any questions that far too often are answered with an adjective or adverb.

Numbers have a sobering effect of reality. If someone asks "How's business"? The response "great!" is the typical answer and that's OK if you're just being polite, but the full answer is left to the judgment of the person asking the question. A more powerful response is one of numbers. How's business? – "Our orders are 20% higher than last year." Notice how much more believable that answer is when numbers are used. Also, note that answers with numbers are expressed in a mode that does not contain a conclusion. The response "great!" is a conclusion, but the comment; "our orders are 20% higher than last year" is a statement of fact and leads the person listening to conclude business is good.

It is also possible to strengthen the credibility depending on how numbers are presented. The believability factor is certainly high when just an actual number is presented. "How's business?" – "We reached $80 million in new orders so far this year." That comment beats responding with "just fine," but this numerical response can be strengthened by comparing it to a standard. For example, "How's business?" "New orders were 20% higher in comparison to last year and reached $80 million." It can become even more credible by adding a prognosis. "How's business?" "New orders were 20% higher in comparison to last year and reached $80 million. This means we will able to retire debt earlier than planned."

Keep in mind the person asking the question is not consciously aware of the power of numerical responses. Hence, they will appear to react no differently than if the question was answered with adjectives or adverbs. However, sub-consciously they feel the difference.

The point is, if you practice responding with numbers, your credibility factor will rise tremendously. It certainly will be higher than a politician who proclaims how "great" he or she will be if elected. You may even want to enter politics once you have mastered the credibility game.

10

Negative Hypotheses

The minds of human beings are very complex and difficult to understand. We are not always sure why we feel a
certain way. Sometimes feelings generate beliefs that are
positive and sometimes negative. Many times our beliefs
are not based on facts, but we nevertheless still have feelings and hence beliefs.

In business, it can be dangerous to harbor beliefs that are
not based on facts, especially if they are negative. I call
these "Negative Hypotheses." They are beliefs based on
feelings and emotions that develop for reasons not quite
known, but are surely not based on facts.

For example, you may believe that the customer service
personnel are not very customer friendly. Your belief is
not based on facts and you're not sure why you feel that
way. That's a negative hypothesis and it must be addressed.
Otherwise, decisions may be made or actions taken that
could be unfair or just plain wrong.

It is, therefore, important to take whatever steps are necessary to eliminate the negative hypothesis. Spend a day with customer service and listen; talk to those who feel the same way you do and seek the factual basis for their feelings. Have conversations with employees who feel favorable about the department, again asking why. The key is to search for facts. Do not let the negative hypotheses linger for any length of time. Try to resolve why you feel the way you do one way or the other. Each day that unexplained feelings are unresolved is a day that a bad decision could be made. Harbor too many negative hypotheses and the possibility for bad decisions increases proportionally.

Feel free to express your negative hypothesis to others. It is after all how you feel and no one can argue with your feelings. You are not saying you are right. It is just a belief that, admittedly, is not based on facts. Make sure everyone knows your belief can be changed if the facts justify such a change.

It is not wrong to have a negative hypothesis. It is wrong to pretend you don't. The brain is complicated. It is the least understood part of the human body. So just run with it. Use the concept of eliminating negative hypotheses and you will be better off.

11

Save A Rug

A dog is a simple creature. It cannot read a job charter nor give feedback signifying acceptance of the owner's expectations. The animal needs to be trained solely by a series of good or bad consequences such that eventually it understands its owner assigned responsibilities. Humans, on the other hand, understand responsibility and are expected to live up to it, but just like a dog if they are not held accountable by a consequence dispensed, it doesn't matter that the human can communicate up front; the assigned responsibility doesn't occur because they are not held accountable.

Responsibility is an assignment and agreement of "expectations." Accountability is a positive or negative "consequence" of achieving or not achieving assigned duties. A positive consequence can be a simple pat on the back, a public announcement of results, granting monetary rewards, giving a promotion, and so forth. Negative consequences can be conveying disappointment or dispensing punishments ranging from job responsibility reductions to out-right terminations. Of course, the most consistent method of administering a consequence is the periodic supervisory review of results and expectations. The point is, there are many forms of consequences some better than others, but they are all consequences.

Without a consequence, the message is clear; the responsibility assigned is not that important. Sure, a responsibility in your work charter could be to keep scrap to less than 1%, but so what if no one measures it, mentions it, or even seems to care. You may internalize a standard for awhile. However, sooner or later, other duties that are actually rewarded if achieved or punished if not, will come to the forefront and those responsibilities that receive no consequences will deteriorate.

Just like training a dog to do their business outside. You tell dogs they are responsible for going outside, but they will ignore you until they feel the consequence of approval for a successful walk or punishment for not waiting.

The word responsibility could be substituted with the word expectations and the word accountability with the word consequence. Neither should exist in a vacuum. If they do, it's no different than having a dog poop on the rug and then experience no consequence. Will the dog continue to poop on the rug? Absolutely! But the sad truth is, so would a human destroy a rug had the parent not praised the toddler for successfully going to the potty. If it's done correctly, you can save the rug.

12

Fat, Dumb, And Happy Is Really Fat, Dumb, And Stupid

Our company is doing just fine, thank you very much. Who are you to suggest we should change our product and how dare you even hint that our service is outdated? We're profitable, aren't we?

When comments like these are made, the company has already started to decline. It is resting on its laurels believing what works today will work tomorrow, while the competition is devising ways of building a better mouse-trap and thinking of improved methods to fulfill the customer's desires.

Profitability does mean something, but look a little deeper. There is a good chance success was related to offering a product just before the market developed. That was their competitive edge. They had it; you wanted it.

That will not last, however. Others out there will certainly notice and want a piece of the action. Some will even create a new competitive advantage.

For example, those businesses that supplied 3- or 5- gallon water jugs to offices made superb profits at one time. The jugs were sold at high margins, delivered, and placed on brown water coolers that were also rented at a high profit. All they had to do was deliver the water jugs in a timely fashion and keep spare cooler units in the warehouse in case a dispensing unit malfunctioned. It was a winner; that is until someone came up with a better mousetrap and offered very attractive sleek water coolers in a choice of 5 colors. That was what the customer really wanted. This new company then had the competitive edge. The fat, dumb, and happy owners and managers of the old company that had a warehouse of ugly brown water coolers ignored the signs and chose not to invest in new equipment. Their sales declined while the company with a new competitive edge flourished.

The owners and managers of the old company were fat, dumb, and happy. In reality they were fat, dumb, and stupid.

13

Give It A Funeral And Move On

Life isn't fair. Accept that concept and you're half way to coping with anything that comes your way.

Too many times people complain about a situation that unfolded and cry "that's not fair." Most of us learned that life isn't fair when we were 3 years old. Indeed, you would be hard pressed to find people who haven't said that to their mothers at least once while they were growing up.

Of course, most of the time the outcry of unfairness is valid, but so what? Accept the reality and expend your energy on those aspects of the future you have a chance of controlling. The odds are you can do little about what just happened and if you could, why spend one more second on the past when the future is just waiting to be conquered? Sure, you should learn from what just happened, but reflect on that while you're attending the funeral you're giving to the unpleasant event.

During my career, I attended an in-house seminar and one participant complained to the group how she was traumatized 5 years earlier when the bank in which she worked as a bank teller, was robbed at gunpoint. She told the group, the event precipitated frequent visits to a psychiatrist. She also proclaimed "no one else in the room could have possibly experienced such horror" and she considered herself extremely unlucky." The group agreed she had experienced a horrible event.

When she finished, I looked around the room and knowing most people's backgrounds, realized there were two well-adjusted people in the room who had had much worse experiences than a bank robbery. The person next to me lost two new-born babies to sudden death syndrome. Another lost his entire family in a gas explosion. Yet these two people never talked about it and certainly didn't dwell on it. They were well adjusted and ready to conquer the world.

Life to these people was certainly unfair just as it was to the victim of a bank robbery, but the bank teller kept living in the past while the others looked to the future. In business, you will experience many unfair events. That's just the way it is. Accept it, learn from it, give it a funeral and move on.

14

The Salami Principle

Twenty-year-old twins Kelly and Belle believed in planning and took it to heart. After college, both Kelly and Belle proclaimed "I want to be a millionaire by the time I'm 40." In short order, each created written plans, listing what they would do with a million dollars, and displayed their plans for all to see. When they turned 40, Kelly was a millionaire but Belle struggled to make ends meet.

So what happened? How can this be? Was Kelly just lucky? Did she win the lottery? The answer to these questions is no of course. Kelly simply used the Salami Principle and Belle did not.

Kelly took her goal of becoming a millionaire and broke it down into time phases. She first sliced the plan (salami) in half, that is, she planned what must be done by the halfway point at age 30. She then sliced that half of the plan in half again, listing what must be accomplished by age 25. She kept slicing the plan in half and planning sub-goals at halfway points, age 22 ½, 21 ¼, and so on until it was sliced to the point where Kelly could list an action step on her daily to-do list.

Kelly could honestly say that her daily to-do list had action steps that, although small, would advance the process to achieving her sub-goals listed at age 21 ¼, 22 ½, 25, 30, and finally at age 40. Kelly sliced the plan (salami) to the point where she knew that as long as she completed the items listed on her daily to-do list, she would eventually achieve the longer-term goal of becoming a millionaire.

Kelly tied it all together; the action items of "Now" to the goal of becoming a millionaire by age 40. Kelly sliced the salami. Belle must have eaten it instead. Come to think about it, she did look a little plump the last time I saw her.

15

Positive Thinking Needs A Daily Dose Of Vitamins

H aving the right positive outlook is fundamental to success. We all know that, but continuously keeping a
positive mental state is a challenge. That takes work and
needs a daily dose of reminders. It is much like vitamins.
You can do just fine without vitamins as long as the food
intake each day is balanced and has all the nutrients required, but that doesn't usually happen and there are a
lot of vitamins sold just to supplement the lack of natural nutrition to help those not eating properly. Indeed if
both the food intake is nutritionally lacking and vitamins
are not digested, more than likely the person will get sick.
It is just a matter of time.

In the business world, you are constantly besieged with
negatives and despite your best intentions to be positive,
it is very easy to succumb mentally to bad news, perceived
unfairness, or a host of unpleasant events that quickly
convert positive thinking into something that's not so

desirable. You are certainly not getting the correct business nutrients you need to sustain a long-term positive
mental state.

That's why vitamins are also necessary for business. I don't
really mean actual vitamins, of course, but I am referring
to vitamins as a metaphor for a dose of positive thinking
reminders that supplement the probable lack of a consistent, positive environment all day long.

Remember, without positive thinking reminders (vitamins) and a business day that lacks consistent positives
(nutrients in food) you will eventually become sick. Not
in a physical way, but in personality and mental states that
are the equivalent of being sick. Indeed, unlike eating
food, a process in which people can control what they
eat and it is possible to eat balanced meals and not need
vitamins, in business, you don't have control of the work
atmosphere and it is a given you won't have a balanced
environment.

That's why positive reminders are critical and fortunately
they are easy to create. Positive reminders can be statements posted on the wall and read every day before you
go to work or a sheet with positive mental reminders that
are on your daily to-do list. They can be questions that
make you reflect on the positives, that is, what are the
good things occurring at work and why? How does that
make you feel? What happened yesterday that made you
happy? What are you enjoying the most in your job right
now and why? How does that make you feel?

Simple stated they are daily reminders; it's just like taking a vitamin pill every day. The only difference is vitamins cost money and positive reminders are totally free. Now that's a deal.

16

Matthew Had A Rolling Stone

There is something about human psychology that makes us become repetitive and repeat the same routine over and over again. We are creatures of habit. That's both good and bad depending on whether the habit helps us or hinders us.

From a practical viewpoint most people have habits that are beneficial such as arriving at work on time, saying hello in the morning, exercising every day and so on. However, the majority also develop bad habits, for example being late on assignments or embellishing factual situations. Habits are like rolling stones; once they start rolling down-hill they keep rolling and rolling. They're hard to stop.

Bad habits, however, can be overcome if a habit builder is created and practiced every day. It is simply a list of bad habits to eliminate. Review the list every day and grade yourself on each item for the previous day's actions. If you can grade your actions as successful (I did not do the bad habit), and record that 20 times in a row, your mind will have been trained and the bad habit is gone. Beware, however, that if on the 12th day, there is a slip up, you must start all over again.

Matthew, for example, had a bad habit of becoming emotional every time even a hint of criticism came his way. He knew that was a bad habit but did it anyway. Matthew wanted to address this weakness. He listed the bad habit on a piece of paper hung it on the side of his desk where no one could see it and every day marked an X if he did anything to stop his emotional tone when criticism occurred. He struggled at first and could not string along 20 times in a row, but eventually he succeeded and trained his mind to break the habit.

Matthew was so happy about eliminating his emotional problem that he decided to analyze himself for other traits he could improve upon. He listed these items on the daily habit list and worked hard to string 20 successes in a row. These bad habits were also eliminated.

In just one year, Matthew's improvements were so pronounced that employees started commenting about how he matured. Some individuals confessed to Matthew that they didn't particularly like him at first, but got accustomed to his style.

Matthew's reaction to these comments was to smile. He knew he didn't mature or that people had adapted to him. Matthew knew he changed on purpose and for the better. Matthew's stone kept rolling along.

17

Never Settle For Mediocrity

Business is a risk and demands a return on investment commensurate with the threat of the investment declining in value. Hence, by the sheer nature of business, that means there should be an expectation of above-average profits relative to all possible investments. The return of an individual business should be better than a less-risky mutual fund comprised of many businesses, better than a government bond, and certainly better than risk-free bank deposits.

It stands to reason, therefore, if a business is only as successful as its people, and due to its inherent risky nature requires superior returns to flourish, then it must also have superior people.

Far too often, however, supervisors settle for average employees and then wonder why the results are mediocre. Investors will only continue to invest in exchange for mediocre returns for a limited time. Eventually, they will take their investment elsewhere.

Granted, it is difficult to heartlessly discount average performers. After all, they get their jobs done reasonably well, they are generally not high maintenance, and they are (in most cases) good people.

Unfortunately, however, a business is not a school, is not a non-profit entity, and as harsh as it seems, it is only required to provide a living to employees who help the entity achieve its relatively superior return on investment goals.

This means an organization needs visionary people who can guide the company out of declining markets into new flourishing areas. It means people are needed who can determine more effective and efficient methods to produce a product or provide a service. It means there must be employees who have the ability to market uniquely and sell day-to-day products better than the competition. It means staff and overhead must keep up with technology to keep costs down.

Now, here is the rub. Average people don't do any of those things. They just do their jobs. They are useful for the short term, but not so good for the long term. Eventually, in time, profits decline as the competitors, who do have superior people, reduce costs, provide better and more appealing mouse traps, and beat the competition. If you are in an organization that appears to be losing to the competition, it probably has far too many mediocre people.

That doesn't mean average people are a problem. More like a bad fit. They can get jobs where the profit motive does not exist and they can thrive. There are plenty of jobs like that in government, for example. The government does not require market positioning and will still continue operating if the service provided isn't up to the same standards as would be tolerated in the private sector.

The harsh reality of a business is that it must earn an acceptable return or it will not continue. A company filled with only average employees will not accomplish superior returns over the long run. It follows, therefore, that a company should "Never settle for mediocrity" or failure is just around the corner.

18

Of Course I'm Ethical

Ask people if they operate ethically and they will answer "of course" and by and large that's correct. However, business ethics is tested every day and it doesn't always come out so cleanly. Troy, for example, accepted an order for 1,000 refrigerators, when he knew full well only 750 were available. The customer made a point to tell Troy that if he did not have 1,000 refrigerators then he would order from a competitor even at a slightly higher price. Troy rationalized that it was better to secure the order and ship 750 refrigerators right away even if the customer was upset, rather than lose the order entirely. He further rationalized that he could later patch it up with the customer.

I can go on with other examples, but it's not necessary, because all questionable ethical behavior has one thing in common: people rationalize their actions. They think, "don't worry about it, I can fix it later" or "feels wrong, but the boss will disapprove if I don't go along." They may think "they owe it to me" or "no one will ever know."

Behaving ethically is always a challenge; however, it can be encouraged by simply asking the following questions:

- Could I explain my actions to my family and feel good about myself?

- Would I be content if my action appeared in the media?

- Would I mind changing places with the person affected and not feel slighted?

- Could I look at myself in the mirror?

If you answer yes to each one of these questions, you're on the right track, but make no mistake about it, it's not an easy task and it is a constant struggle. Therefore, the next time someone asks you if you're ethical you should answer "I strive to be ethical every day." You can never simply say "Of Course."

19

Clairvoyance And The Organizational Span Of Control

Look at any company's organization chart and, without talking to anyone in the company, it is possible to determine with a high degree of accuracy where moral problems exist between subordinates and supervisors. Sound clairvoyant? It's not.

The number one reason for tension between two levels in an organization is not lack of recognition or appreciation or low pay, but an improper set up of the organizational span of control in the first place.

Span of Control means simply the number of people reporting to a boss. It can vary depending on circumstances, but if it is either too low or too high, morale problems will inevitably arise.

That being said, organizations should logically strive for the optimal span of control. However, that's easier said than done because much subjectivity goes into the equation.

The optimal span of control depends on a job's degree of complexity and the magnitude of interaction needed with the boss. If a job involves solving non-routine problems, there is a good chance the boss will get involved. Therefore, the frequency of day-to-day interactions, between a supervisor and the subordinate is high. From the supervisor's standpoint, it will take time to manage this subordinate. Conversely, if the job is routine and needs very little hand holding the supervisor will spend very little with the subordinate.

It stands to reason, therefore, if a subordinate's responsibility entails low levels of maintenance by the supervisor, for example a production worker on a manufacturing line, then the production line supervisor should be able to manage a broad number of subordinates because each position requires low levels of the supervisor's attention. The opposite is true for a general manager, who must supervise department heads who require high maintenance due to their job complexities of running a department.

For example, a production line supervisor can manage fifteen production line employees and be just fine but a general manager may struggle with more than seven department heads as direct reports. Now watch what happens when the maximum is violated. Let's say the production line supervisor has 50 production line workers instead of the comfortable fifteen. Under these circumstances, the production line supervisor becomes swamped and is prone to making errors as he or she is forced to skim over problems. This in turn brings pressure from his or her boss, who is also not happy with errors. The production line supervisor becomes uneasy and irritable; his or her subordinates sense this tone and many avoid interaction. Others don't read the stressed climate and are in the boss's face about trivial matters. The trivial matters get the boss's time and attention; the more important matters take a lower priority because they are not surfacing as they should. Certainly, under these circumstances, relationships are not growing between two layers in the organizational hierarchy.

Issues can also arise when the span of control does not have enough direct reports. If the general manager had only two direct reports, instead of a reasonable seven, he or she would have a boring job. That's because the general manager will have a disproportionately lower number of issues involving his or her time. Sometimes managers will find themselves in that position and will take advantage of it by becoming lazy, but the vast majorities of people are not lethargic and instead occupy their time getting involved in areas in which they shouldn't. General Managers with only two direct reports will start interacting directly with the next layer below their two direct reports. The two direct reports will either object outright or allow their boss to go around them without going through the chain of command. For example, let's say the general manager is feeling bored and starts scheduling the production line (which is the responsibility of his subordinate, the operations manager). The bored general manager works directly with a layer below his subordinate the operations manager. In time, the operations manager may not feel responsible even though it is one part of his or her job responsibilities. That's okay initially, but the operations manager might eventually realize that the boss, the general manager, is not good at scheduling and production targets may not be met. The operations manager uses the scheduling flaws as an excuse, but his or her boss the general manager will not accept this. The operations manager feels caught in the middle and becomes frustrated. The general manager also becomes unhappy and starts believing that the operations manager is not a good performer. The end result is ill-will again between two organizational layers simply because the span of control was violated.

That brings us back to the opening question: Is it possible to determine morale problems in a company by simply reviewing the organization chart and finding violations in the span of control? The answer is absolutely yes and arriving at the answer doesn't require clairvoyance. Just look for violations in the principles of a proper span of control. If it's not set up properly, there is a good chance a problem exists. Fix it, but beware: people may think you are clairvoyant, like Jeanne Dixon or Nostradamus. Just smile quietly, knowing it's all legit.

20

Leona Was An Ornery Cuss But Had An Achilles Heel

Leona would tell people in no uncertain terms to toe the line. She would lean into people and with a loud voice, speak her mind. She was a dominating woman and overpowered everyone. Her style was that of a bully.

Her problem, however, was that she wasn't particularly liked; she was feared, and because of her pushy mannerisms never got close to anyone.

Eventually, Leona stopped listening to people. After all, it was much easier simply to overpower whoever got in her way. It was one-way communication and, of course, she did not obtain the typical feedback that most people receive. It wasn't very long before many of her actions and decisions were routinely incorrect.

Leona eventually became destructive to the Company. Her associates preferred to let her frequent bad decisions just go unchallenged. No one wanted to address a bully. Her own boss was intimidated by her and let her get away with poor performance.

One day the boss hired Alinda, who could see right through Leona and was not intimidated by her bully style. Alinda was so successful at dealing with Leona that fellow employees noticed. Tyler in particular was amazed at how effectively she handled Leona and asked her for a few pointers. Alinda was more than happy to teach him.

Alinda's advice to Tyler was first and foremost address the power of Leona with even greater power right back at her. Answer every condescending question of Leona's with an even more condescending question. Talk bold, lean into her, look her in the eye and win the battle of domination.

Alinda went on to say it works because Leona is not accustomed to such actions and she doesn't know how to react to them. Leona has an Achilles heel, namely more powerful people who will put her in her place.

Hey Leona, what goes around comes around.

21

Buffoons Can Be Funny - Or Not

During medieval times, buffoons assumed the roles of clowns, court jesters, and entertainers who were laughed at. A buffoon was never taken seriously. Yet, just about everyone at work has at some time been treated as a buffoon.

Buffoon treatment can come in the form of a chuckle when a comment is made with the purpose of denigrating the commenter. It might come in the form of people who roll their eyes, as if what was just said is ridiculous, even if the comment was totally valid. It can be verbal comments such as, "What were you thinking" or "that makes no sense." All are assaults and each is implying you are a buffoon.

People who treat their fellow humans this way have both security issues and evil streaks that should not go unchecked. The good news, buffoon treatment can be caught and easily handled.

The first trick is to spot the occurrence as it happens. Be cognizant of both the non-verbal and verbal signs. Resist the natural inclination to laugh when you're being laughed at. Pause for one second and reflect on what just happened. Then, and only then, after silence is in the air, repeat and highlight for the perpetrator exactly what his or her actions are doing. For example, when people roll their eyes respond directly to them and reveal you noticed them rolling their eyes. Politely mention how rolling your eyes is disrespectful and usually happens when people try to avoid discussing the merits of a subject. Or, as another example, If someone says, "that makes no sense" and makes the condescending "huh" sound while making a contorted, disapproving face, repeat back to them how their comment and accompanying facial expressions seem to be a broad-brush dismissal of your comment. Specifically ask if that is done on purpose hoping to escape discussing your idea?

The next time you go to a medieval fair and see the buffoonery of a court jester, remember he's funny on purpose. That's his or her job. However, that's never the case at work; if you allow someone to treat you like a buffoon and they succeed, then you are one and you deserve it. Indeed, you may want to change careers. I hear that Renaissance Fairs are always looking for talent.

22

Be Aware Of The Porcupine

Porcupines are not animals you would choose as pets. They are not particularly friendly, look weird, and petting them is problematic. Although, we don't fear them the way we fear lions or tigers, we certainly don't feel comfortable around them. After all, every time you deal with a porcupine, you tend to get pricked.

In the work environment, you may run into a "porcupine." They don't walk on all fours and they look just like us. After all, they are human. But make no mistake about it, they are porcupines in disguise. They get results but at the price of pricking people as they go about their business. Granted they don't shoot off 10 porcupine needles at a time. More like a needle here and a needle there randomly dispersed, but they nevertheless make people feel uncomfortable. Indeed, this gradual piercing approach is so subtle that most of the time the people being pricked don't even realize it. They just know they don't feel right.

Porcupines need to be identified quickly because their ability to get results will only last at best 6 months, after which they actually become counterproductive. That's because many employees avoid porcupines as they get tired of feeling uncomfortable around them. Others realize they are being pricked and that angers them. Eventually, everyone stops cooperating with the porcupine. The porcupine begins to throw off two needles at a time and almost everyone starts to protest. In time, too much energy is spent on discussing the porcupine's problems. Arguments and confrontations occur and productivity suffers.

The bottom line is porcupines should not be part of business. Don't be tempted to salvage these types of people. Their traits were developed during their childhood and were ingrained. Only many years of psychological help would fix them and that is a cost a company should not be required to endure.

Let's face it: porcupines are not men's or women's best friend.

23

Blood Is Thicker Than Water

It's natural for parents to worry about their kids and to help them in this cruel world. It's also natural for siblings to develop an unbreakable bond so strong their own kids have a special relationship (as cousins) with each other. After all, offspring are in an elite relationship club and all are loved. They are blood.

It is safe to say that feelings for blood relatives transcend everything. That's why it is a big mistake to hire people that are related to someone in the company. Indeed, as soon as a person related to someone considered important is hired, the unrelated employees' objective thinking and rational actions go haywire. That's because unrelated employees recognize the special relationship and will not only disproportionately help the related party but also significantly reduce any challenges that would typically be made to non-related parties. Just how disruptive it may be, depends on the highest position held by the related parties. The higher the position of either party the greater the impact.

It is hard to condemn anyone who is simply trying to help a blood relative. The ironic twist, however, is that over the long haul nepotism does just the opposite. When two blood relatives are employed in the company, the lowest level relative is in a protective bubble and does not learn life lessons. If that bubble bursts because the higher level relative loses his or her job it is like sending a lion cub, that was nurtured by humans, out into the jungle.

For example, if Linda, the Vice President Marketing of Jim B Enterprises Inc., hires Ellery her daughter, Ellery will not truly be held accountable if she performs poorly, unlike all other unrelated employees. Oh, Linda may say "treat my daughter like everyone else," but everyone knows she isn't like everyone else. Ellery has direct access to Linda the VP Marketing. Employees will quite naturally be intimidated and even convince themselves that Ellery is performing OK when she is not. Even if Ellery is performing fine, it may be because she gets undo attention. Her requests, for example, receive immediate responses, or she receives lavish help non-related employees would not be given. That's a problem because Ellery, like a lion cub raised by humans, is not learning how to influence people for actions desired, is not learning how to generate her own clout so people take her seriously, and is not preparing herself for the probable jungle that will come to her sometime in the future when her mother is out of the picture.

Keep in mind, the blood relative need not be the Vice President of Marketing of the company. It could be anyone in a high enough position that non-blood employees perceive the related person as possessing the ability to impact them either negatively or positively within the organization. Even in the case of two blood relatives of equal stature, the non-blood employees may one-day need to contend with firing one that which, in turn, may cause the other to quit.

The phrase "Blood is Thicker than Water" has been around for quite some time. That's because love is blind. It is one of the greatest aspects of human life, but it does not belong in business.

24

Whack-A-Mole

Did you ever play Whack-a-Mole at a fair? It's a game of concentration and reflexes. The objective of the game is to hit the mole when it pops up from pretend holes in the ground. Sounds easy, and it would be except there are many of these holes and the mole may pop up from any one of them. To make it even more challenging they only stay up for a fraction of a second.

Some people are good at Whack-a-Mole and frequently win. Others are not as skilled in comparison. Good or bad, however, everyone enjoys whacking that mole. Even little kids who haven't yet developed fast enough reflexes and seem to be just a fraction of a second off, enjoy it so much that they will beg to play again.

In the workplace, the game Whack-a-Mole exists. For example, the mole could be that old entrance awning that fell down in a heavy snow storm. Many people said the awning was in bad shape and warned that a heavy snow could cause it to collapse. Even the person responsible for building maintenance said the same thing. Yet nothing was done.

But watch how fast the damaged awning gets fixed now that it is on the ground and poses a safety problem for people entering work. Mr. Maintenance, like a bolt of lightning, rounds up the necessary equipment, detaches the badly damaged awning from the building, arranges for a new awning that he personally rushes to the store to buy, and then installs it within hours of the incident.

It is amazing. People applaud him, praise his speedy response, and know deep down there is no way they could have pulled off that rescue operation as fast as he accomplished it. Mr. Maintenance is extremely good at Whack-a-Mole. The mole was the awning and he whacked it back into the hole with authority. When all was said and done, he loved those feelings of recognition and took pride in his Whack-a-Mole skill.

In business, however, these Whack-a-Mole skills are only occasionally needed in true unplanned emergencies. Most of the time relying on Whack-a-Mole skills can be a problematic. Case in point: the awning should never have fallen down in the first place. Mr. Maintenance should have determined the likelihood of the awning becoming a safety hazard and fixed it before it became a problem. He should have gone underneath the surface to determine why the moles keep popping their heads up and he should have eliminated the moles. Mr. Maintenance instead chose to wait until the awning fell down, at which time he was able to show off his Whack-a-Mole skills. A truly effective employee would have resisted the temptation to wait for a problem to develop and instead fixed the situation before it became an emergency. Over the long haul, these effective people get (hopefully) the best recognition of all, a promotion.

Whack-a-Mole is fun, but in business reliance on these skills can be counterproductive. After all, that awning could have fallen down on employees and whacked them in the head, or maybe even hit an innocent "mole" bystander.

25

Whatever

You've heard it many times, "whatever you say," "sure whatever," or just plain "whatever." The word *whatever* is a favorite among people who want to dismiss you, weaken what you say, or get you out of their hair quickly. It is an insult, a verbal slap and a way of responding to a person without actually responding. It's an attempt to cut you off. It absolutely puts up a wall between any two people and halts any progress in communicating.

If you could halt time in its tracks and analyze what just took place when the word *whatever* was used, you would realize it was someone saying you're not important, that they do not have time for your nonsense so leave them alone. It is one of the most disrespectful words in the English language.

You could respond by saying "whatever," but then you become precisely the person you should try not to be.

The word *whatever* should be banned in your organization. By the way don't show this chapter to your spouse, he or she may disagree, storm out of the room and say "whatever."

26

No Need To Punish Baseball Players

Rod Carew, a major league baseball player, was great at his trade. He had a lifetime batting average of .328, was a MVP, and was voted to the All Star team 18 times. Yet during his entire career he never received a performance appraisal. Why not, after all playing baseball is a job isn't it? He gets paid a salary. Then why not give Rod a formal performance appraisal just like everyone else who has a job?

Well, the truth is baseball doesn't use performance appraisals. Indeed, the thought of sitting down with a baseball player and completing an annual formal written performance appraisal and then discussing improvement areas before filling the sheet in the personnel file is just considered silly.

Yet baseball is a job and all jobs need a basic appraisal of performance. So why is baseball an exception? Because in baseball, management has mastered the fundamental part of the appraisal process missed by most businesses.

In baseball "every player" knows the answer to two signifi-cant questions and therefore, receives an appraisal on a continual basis, not just once a year.

Question #1 - What is specifically required of me?

Question #2 - How do I know I am doing a good job?

Question #1 is used to ask, "why I am being paid?" In Rod Carew's case, why am I being paid so much? The answer, of course, is contributing to the team's winning by achieving at least last year's stats; batting .300 or more, being an MVP candidate, and making the all star team. How does Rod Carew know he is contributing to wins and how does he know he is performing in the manner expected of him? That is question number 2. In baseball, these two questions can be answered easily. Statistics have historically demonstrated that if a player has a high bat-ting average and makes the all star team his team wins more games. Rod knows this and he is paid a high salary because management relies upon him to achieve at least, last year's high stats. No one needs to tell him that. These expectations are so engrained in his head, in his bosses' heads, and with the fans as they watch his stats on the screen every time Rod comes up to bat, that they are a given. If Rod bats .240 he knows he is not performing up to expectations. Rod punishes himself. His boss need not review his performance and tell him he needs to improve and can, instead, spend time encouraging and helping Rod get better.

Now contrast this to a typical business job. There is no huge screen that flashes results to give instant feedback to employees. The majority of employees don't know what is expected of them and how to know if they are doing a good job. They don't have a batting average, slugging percentage, or fielding stats. Many employees can't directly associate their action to contributing to the company winning games, or in business terms, making a profit. Indeed most companies don't even tell the employees if the game was won or lost (profit achieved to plan) and some go out of their way to hide it.

The only recourse most bosses have is to sit down with their subordinates once a year and judgmentally assess performance. The boss will pull out the form and evaluate whether the subordinate behaved in a positive manner, was a team player, and so forth. If the business is a little more advanced, its performance appraisal process may include assessments of the Operations Manager's achievements in manufacturing widgets, or the number of tasty meals prepared by the Head Chief based on surveys. The boss will tell the subordinate that he or she was weak in certain areas. Many times employees are finding out for the first time and that puts the boss is in a punishment mode.

However, this is non-sense; every business job can be just like baseball players. Expectations can be spelled out in detail and measurements devised for each expectation so the employee knows for sure how they are being measured. Department or company results can be equated to wins so everyone can celebrate victories as they happen, just like in baseball. Bosses can be like baseball coaches. They never need to punish subordinates for not performing because the expected results are so clear and published for all to see, that the employees will punish themselves. The employees not only feel part of the team but also know how they contribute to team victories. There is only one problem that you need to worry about; you may find you have a sudden craving for peanuts and crackerjacks.

27

Lions, Gazelles, And African Wild Dogs

The main goal of lions, which are at the top of the food chain, is survival. They understand that they must have food or they will die. That's why lions are one of the most focused animals in the world when on the hunt. When lions are hungry and see a tasty gazelle, they perk up and go after the meal like a laser focused on a target. After all, their goal is to fill up their bellies and survive.

However, watch closely and notice that lions will charge after their meals with so much focus that they fail to see anything else, even if a bigger and tastier second gazelle is running right alongside. Instead, lions will keep on charging after the first gazelle and ignore an even easier-to-catch second gazelle. To lions, that's not a problem because most of the times they catch the first gazelle and consequently manage to live with full bellies. They know they are "kings of the jungle" and at the top of the food chain; they can get the gazelle that got away sometime later. That's why lions can be focused and need not concern themselves with anything else that comes along.

This is not true for African Wild Dogs. They will stop for the second gazelle that's running alongside the pack because they worry about inadvertently running into dangerous lion territory and becoming the hunted.

Note that neither lions nor African wild dogs will stop their hunts to munch on a much smaller animal. Either could easily pounce on a little animal and eat it, but it won't make a dent in quenching their hunger. The gazelle would get away and both lions and wild dogs would eventually starve.

Clearly, then, the lion is better off staying totally focused rather than getting sidetracked, even with a bigger and tastier gazelle that's running right alongside. It is also clear the lion should never even consider stopping for a much smaller animal. They are, after all, on top of the food chain. That is only partially true for African wild dogs that must compete for food with lions. The African wild dog must watch for animals nearby while still focusing on the gazelle. The African wild dog will only pass up the much smaller animal.

In the business world, no one is king of the jungle. Business people are more like African wild dogs. Sure, staying focused to achieve a goal is paramount to success, but unlike the lion, and more like a wild dog, employees can't afford to let unforeseen opportunities (the gazelle running alongside) go unnoticed. Of course, no one should get sidetracked on less important matters (i.e. the smaller animal) and everyone must stay focused on the main goal (filling up the belly). Remember, you are not king of the jungle and it is appropriate to watch for a second gazelle that may run alongside. After all, the first gazelle may take longer to catch, get away, and you may find yourself without food. Even worse become the food to competitors. It is a risk a business should not take.

Lions must be strong to survive; business people, much like wild dogs, must be both strong and smart to stay alive. You may not like it, but it is a jungle out there. Maybe in your next life you will be re-incarnated as a lion.

28

Patience Is A Virtue

Funding employee education, contributing to the American Cancer Society, hiring the handicapped, following environmental conservation practices, and helping the disadvantaged are all marvelous social goals. Just like any expenditure in a business, however, they must always be ranked and compared to other expenditures before the actual release of funds.

Social expenses must be compared to the cost of the products sold or services performed, and to the cost of acquiring the revenue stream in the first place. These required expenditures will always take precedence over social costs. Social expenses are always precluded from competing with critical costs that keep the business running. That leaves just overhead to compete against.

However, tell that to anyone who is listed in the overhead category and you will get a convincing argument why overhead is also absolutely necessary to keep the business machine humming. Assuming this is true, that leaves social expenses in the lurch and unable to compete with any expenditure. Social costs must instead compete only if revenue is greater than expenditures. Simply speaking, a profit must first happen and be large enough that an investor in the business reaps a return high enough not to disinvest.

Only a consistent stream of earnings will provide the possibility to even consider making expenditures that are not essential to making an adequate profit return. Without profits, there is simply nothing to give to the environmental causes or other social projects. Without profits, investors will liquidate and those who have been pushing for social causes will lose their jobs and not be in a position to push any longer.

If a business is not successful because it has succumbed to the temptation of providing social expenditures when profits were not achieved, it will have violated the core fundamental capitalistic principle that a business exists to bring an adequate return to investors. It is far better to sponsor more social causes during times of high profit and very little when profits are nonexistent than always contribute no matter what the profit circumstances. Those companies that contribute for social concerns only when profits allow will live much longer than those companies that always contribute during both good and bad times. The disciplined, longer-lived company will ultimately spend more on social programs over time.

Therefore, the social conscience employee's primary goal should always be to make a profit first; then help the social causes. Those employees fighting for social needs will be much happier if patience is exhibited. So, too, will those well-deserving organizations and unfortunate disadvantaged individuals that depend on corporate funds.

Short-term, inopportune pressure to contribute to social causes will result in less social funding than striking while profits are hot. Patience is certainly a virtue.

29

Rose No Longer Needed Rose-Colored Glasses

Sarah and Bobbi worked at the same company and sold equine buildings for a living. Their day consisted of responding to leads received, meeting the prospective customers at construction sites to discuss their building needs, and hopefully convincing them their buildings were better than the competitor's. The price was important, but generating a feeling of confidence with the prospective customer was even more important.

Sarah would sell her share of equine buildings each year, but Bobbi would sell at least double that amount and was the number 1 salesperson year after year. Their boss, Linda Rose, always looked at the sales results with rose-colored glasses and deemed Sarah's low performance acceptable. One day, however, Linda Rose got tired of accepting the status quo and was determined to understand why Bobbi was so much better than Sarah. Hence, Linda Rose went on sales calls with both Sarah and Bobbi and recorded the sales pitches each made. When Linda Rose went back to the office, she played the recordings over and over again dissecting each salesperson's approach and analyzing every inflection made. Linda Rose was determined to understand why Bobbi was so much more successful than Sarah.

Linda Rose's initial assessment was that both Sarah and Bobbi did an excellent job pitching the building sale to their respective customers, which left Linda Rose even more perplexed. Still determined, she dug in a little further and studied every word that was said. Finally, as if a bolt of lightning struck her, she realized there was one big difference between Sarah and Bobbi. Sarah used qualifiers and Bobbi did not. Sarah would say "if" frequently. The prospective customer would ask "Can the building be built by the end of September?" Sarah would reply, "yes, if everything happens as planned." Bobbi would reply, "yes, we will make sure everything happens as planned." Sarah used a qualifier and Bobbi did not. Although it was not a big difference in the overall word content, it made a huge difference in how confident the prospective customer felt. Sarah, by using the word "if" was already playing the blame game. She set conditions and was fortifying herself against potential failure. Bobbi, on the other hand, was assuming a successful outcome.

That wasn't all; Linda Rose also noticed that Sarah used words like "I guess" while Bobbi never did. Sarah, without realizing it, was indirectly saying she wanted leeway to claim later "I didn't really know, I was only guessing." The words "I guess" do not exude confidence. In addition, Sarah used the words "try" and "maybe," but Bobbi did not. When Sarah said "try" she was implying to the customer that she had no intentions of doing what the prospective customer requested. When she used "maybe" the prospective customer felt Sarah was non-committal and that caused feelings of doubt.

The next day, armed with her new-found enlightenment, Linda Rose helped Sarah improve. After a few months, Sarah sold 75% more and was jubilant. Bobbi, on the other hand, became concerned since Sarah was now competing for the number 1 salesperson spot. Bobbi was forced to step up her game.

The happiest person was Linda Rose the boss. She now had two high performing individuals in her department. Linda Rose's glasses were no longer rose-colored any-more. Linda Rose could see clearly without any tint and, of course, qualifiers were never used in her department again.

30

Watch Out! A Five-Year-Old May Beat You At Chinese Checkers

Did you ever play Chinese checkers? It is a board game shaped like a star; five-year-olds and up can play. The goal of the game is to be the first to move a set of marbles from holes on one side of the board to holes on the other side. You are allowed to jump over other marbles in play, which moves your marbles faster to the other side. The trick is to move all the marbles simultaneously with single, double, and triple jumps rather than advancing one hole at a time.

Business is just like Chinese checkers. It is best not to work on one task at a time but instead juggle a dozen or so activities all at once. Real progress occurs by planning the completion of your tasks in such a way that efficiency occurs as you implement.

This means don't just talk to Jake about the requirements of the new scheduling system if there are three other areas needing Jake's involvement. Be prepared to discuss all tasks simultaneously and advance each of the tasks together.

Treat business like Chinese checkers. Work on tasks concurrently. Remember, it is just like jumping multiple marbles. If you do not, you will never beat those who do, and yes, that includes five-year-olds.

31

No Decision Is A Decision But

Good Luck With That

You're presented with a problem, but not sure what to do. It's your time to be decisive. Deep down you know you should decide, but it's difficult to act. You know that everybody is willing to state their opinion, provided there is no negative liability bestowed upon them. However, that's not true for you.

When put in this scenario, most people make no decision. They ask for more analysis. They say, "let me think about it." They often simply ignore it. That's because being decisive often means "putting your money (career or reputation) where your mouth is." It involves willingness to risk failure, ridicule, and the possibility of having to force the issues on someone who disagrees.

Making no decision means something else will eventually happen, but more times than not it will be the wrong something. Blockbuster Video, for example, had plenty of opportunities to divest of its video stores and enter into new markets where technology was progressing, but could not make that decision. There were many discussions, but a concrete decision was not made. Months went by, much analysis was prepared, but no definitive decision resulted. In the meantime, other companies recognized this technology shift and acted quickly. They were decisive. These companies took market share and significantly benefited while Blockbuster was less decisive and lost out.

Now, it is not always the case that no decision results in a negative. After all, you can get lucky. However, not making a decision means you are just hoping for the best. That may work, but it is a risky way to run a business. Good luck with that.

32

Never Use The N Word

The N word is vulgar, divisive, creates unnecessary tension, and diverts action away from progress where it belongs. Yet, it is constantly used in the workplace. OK, then why doesn't management stop it or just forbid it totally, especially considering how damaging it can be? Well, simply stated that's because most employees don't understand nor realize when they are saying it.

The N word is like heart disease, a silent killer except you can hear it. It comes in many different forms in varying degrees and doesn't necessarily start with the letter N. Nevertheless, it is crippling in a business environment.

I am referring, of course, to the word "No." The word no is used almost every day. It is a method of stopping behavior unwanted by the person saying it. The problem with using No is that it is very disrespectful. It's a lazy person's way of cutting short an explanation of the merits of not moving forward. The person who is saying No might as well say "I don't have time to explain why we shouldn't proceed," or "you're just not important enough for me to explain why I feel that way."

Using No is also one of the biggest deflators of ideas. It is the quickest way to stop suggestions in their tracks. Walt Disney refused to accept no for an answer and he arguably had more bad ideas than good ones, but no one was allowed to say no to him. If Walt's approach made little sense, his team was then forced to describe the reasons for taking another approach, and the amazing end result was that Walt's staff not only explained the problem of proceeding with Walt's view but also came up with alternative and better solutions.

The word no comes in many forms, "That won't work," "We tried that before," "You've got to be kidding," and so on. When these phrases are heard, immediately challenge the person saying No and demand a justifiable explanation and an alternative solution.

The employee may cry out that it takes too much time to justify a no answer and serves little purpose, but is that really true? How often have people's brains been turned off just because they feel they will get a disrespectful no answer? How many ideas were lost because the no word was allowed to flourish? What idea surfaced that could have made the company more profitable but was never pursued?

The "no" word (or as I referred to it at the start of this chapter to get your attention: the N word) should be eliminated. The other N word, of course, should never be tolerated as it is a much higher willful form of hatred and disrespect.

33

Control Little Tommy But Empower

His Friends

If a group of 5-year-old kids play in an open field where they have never been before, patterns emerge. The group will play many games of course, but they will not play Hide & Seek. That's because they don't feel comfortable enough with the surroundings. They are apprehensive and unsure if they have permission to go 100 yards away and hide behind a nearby tree. Therefore, almost all 5-year-olds will play within a circle that is maybe 20 yards in diameter. That is, except, for little Tommy; he seems to have no fear and dashes far away from the group deep into the woods. That's a problem, of course, because now the chaperone must stop everything and find little Tommy.

Now, put a fence around the field (and include some trees) and watch what the 5-year-olds do. They no longer play within the 20-yard circle. Instead, they move about freely knowing they must stay within the fence, which gives them comfort. They spread out more and play different games. Some 5-year-olds start playing the game they like most: Hide & Seek. There are smiles on their faces. They are growing. Additionally, little Tommy is safe now within the confines of the fence.

The same is true in the business world. Whether you are the CEO of a company, in charge of the department, or in a staff position with no subordinates, all organizations should make it very clear to you who has authority for approving important transactions and decisions. It's like putting up a fence around the field. It should be positioned to empower employees to make decisions without worry of being second-guessed while simultaneously placing constraints on the little Tommy's of the world who might put the company at risk.

Failure to establish defined authorizations leads employees huddling in small circles, letting decisions rise to higher levels, and taking the risk of a few rogue renegades running off and doing damage. It stands to reason, therefore, that some controls are definitely needed. However, just how much and how little control is established is paramount. Controls that are too tight may stop the little Tommy's of the world, but do very little to enable everyone else. It would be like putting a fence in a 20-yard circle. Conversely, controls too broad can expose the company to the consequences of bad decisions made by inadequately trained employees. When a fence is placed 2 miles into the woods, little Tommy can still get lost.

The factors that influence your decision to place tight and loose controls should reflect the amount of damage that can be done to the organization by the Tommy types. By far, the main considerations should be to empower all others to the extent of their proven abilities and allow individual growth. Tommy can be counseled separately to be a team player. If he responds, great, if he does not, cut him loose. The other employees should get your attention. You never know who will be the next Lee Iacocca.

34

Don't Kick The Dog

Did you ever find yourself in a bad mood and didn't know why? Well, join the club. It happens in spite of all your efforts to stay in a positive frame of mind. How you handle it once it occurs, however, is critical.

Some people kick their dog. Oh, I don't mean physically kicking their dog, but I do mean treating their dog badly. They do this because no matter how bad they treat their dog, the dog takes it and forgives whatever they did.

At work, there is a temptation to do the same with those people with whom you feel comfortable. If you succumb, you are kicking the dog. Sure, you're forgiven because they rationalize that you're just in a bad mood and everything is OK when you are in a good mood.

It is, however, not OK. There is no excuse for kicking your subordinates, fellow associates or anyone in any capacity no matter what mood you're in, and it is particularly bad to kick anyone that responds to you in the same fashion a dog would.

What is important to remember is that just because the person was OK with your disrespect doesn't mean they will always be OK with it. At some point, the cumulative disrespect reaches a point of no return and your fellow associate begins to dislike you even when you're in a good mood.

Never kick the dog. If you do, your future relationships with those you're most comfortable with can only go downhill. Sure, humans don't bite, but they could do much worse: both disrespect and dislike you forever.

35

For Every Problem Bring Two Recommendations For A Solution "The Two Recommendation Rule"

A supervisor always feels great when a subordinate asks a question. You may hear the boss say, "That's why they pay me the big bucks." That sounds logical, but it's all driven by ego and its all bull.

A supervisor's job is to get the job done by holding people accountable to responsibilities, motivating, delegating, and performing all those management necessities that go with it. That doesn't mean the boss shouldn't roll up his or her sleeves, but it does mean maximizing the developing talents of subordinates.

That's not going to happen if every time a question is asked by a subordinate, an answer is given by the boss. Answering every question for subordinates creates drones and it robs them of the opportunity to improve, to develop, and eventually to be promoted. It shuts off the brain and the analytical thinking necessary for success.

This is where the "Two Recommendation Rule" comes into play. If you're the boss just require two recommendations for solutions. If you are the subordinate then give two recommendations for solutions. Not one, but two recommendations. Granted, it is hard to come up with one recommendation, let alone two, but requiring two recommendations will guarantee that the mind is open and analyzing the situation.

I remember when I took over a new job. It was apparent my predecessor answered every question for his subordinates. I knew this because on the very first day on the job there was a parade of people coming into my office asking, "How does this procedure work?" or "How do I do fix this problem?" It was a real challenge. I remember asking myself, "Why would they believe anyone would know the answer to procedural questions on the first day on the job?" It certainly highlighted the fact that their brains were turned off, mainly because their former boss answered every question they had.

I knew this was not the best way to maximize results, so I immediately put up a sign outside my office that read "For every problem bring me two recommendations for a solution." At first, everyone ignored it and kept asking unnecessary questions. When this happened, I would ask each person for his or her two recommendations. If they didn't have any, I would tell each to return when they were prepared to give two recommendations and sent them back to where they came from. Eventually everyone returned, but this time followed the "Two Recommendation Rule." Amazingly, as the days passed, the line outside the office got smaller and smaller. What happened was remarkable; requiring two recommendations opened up their minds and it became silly to bother me once they realized they had the answer all along. My time was freed up to pursue more important areas and my subordinates were much better decision makers. They were certainly much closer to promotions.

36

Follow Mary Poppins' Spoonful Of Sugar Rule

Mary Poppins was right: a spoonful of sugar does make the medicine go down.

Mary Poppins was also smart. She knew the best way to address a negative, was to introduce a positive simultaneously.

For example, Jeff has a poor habit of interrupting others and you want to correct it. Therefore, don't "just" ask him to stop interrupting; also compliment Jeff on his ability to create smiles from others (that is, until he interrupts).

Jeff will, of course, have mixed feelings about what you just said, but the positive comment about valuing his ability to produce smiles will soften the negative aspect of bringing up the issue of interrupting.

Some call it the Mary Poppins' Spoonful of Sugar Rule. It works extremely well, especially while completing an employee appraisal in which negatives are inevitably discussed.

Follow Mary Poppins' lead and you will find it's not that difficult to address improvements. It also has the wonderful side effect of seeking the positives in a person in order to counter the negatives.

There is one exception to the Mary Poppins rule. If you truly can't come up with one positive to counteract the negative, this person is in the wrong movie. Politely give directions to where a more sinister film is being shot and forget about dispensing sugar with the medicine entirely.

37

Hang With Positive Patty Shun Debbie Downer

Who you hang with, associate with, and/or confide in is a choice made every day.

It is one of the most important choices you can make for both happiness in life and progress in business. That's why you must assess both your friends and business associates. Sure, it's difficult and possibly painful; however, the person you thought was your friend may after further reflection, not be a friend at all. The same is true of a business associate. It takes soul-searching and know-how to spot the good, the bad, or the ugly.

The key is to watch for clues. Is your friend or business associate Debbie Downer or Positive Patty? Is she truly happy when good things happen to you or silently giving you the obligatory minimum nod and acknowledgement?

For example, after Brian was promoted, Positive Patty may say, "that's wonderful" and ask all about Brian's situation. No doubt she probably was the one who encouraged him in the first place. Debbie Downer, on the other hand, would say "if you become a supervisor you will be one of those," or "now that you were promoted you probably will have new friends." Debbie's comments are not uplifting and are subtly bringing Brian down. Debbie believes that misery loves company and if she can't succeed then true friends shouldn't either. Debbie Downer would rationalize that true friends should stick together to keep from being lonely at the bottom.

Positive Patty doesn't try to convert you. She is just happy that good things have happened to you. Debbie Downer, on the other hand, is actually trying to change you to a Debbie Downer. Like a devil from below, sign that contract with Debbie Downer and you might as well change your name to Debbie, and if you're a man that's really a downer.

38

Take The Bull By The Horns And Charge

How many times have you heard someone say, "I don't have the authority to do my job" or "When are they going to grant me the authority I need?" What absolute crap! The day you started work authority has already been granted and each day thereafter is earned one step at a time.

Forget the misperception that authority must be expressly and routinely granted. Your job charter which lists your responsibilities is the basis of your authority and presumed given unless specifically told otherwise. Sure, job charters are sometimes too general or don't exist at all and if that is the case, create one so it becomes the badge you can show if your actions are challenged.

Authority doesn't happen the second you begin working. It is earned one step at a time. Stay focused on your job charter. Ask, "will the actions I am about to take help achieve my business responsibilities as I perceive the role of my job charter?" Also ask, "will I be in compliance with published delegation of authority documents and with any expressed requests from my supervisor?" If the answer is yes, why are you waiting? Take the bull by the horns and charge.

39

Bananas, Apples, & Raisins Oh My –

"The Bar Rule"

Managing inventory can be a difficult task. Too much inventory and cash is squeezed. Too little and sales may be lost. That's why almost all companies track inventory turns by SKU's and also order goods in the most economic quantities. Many companies have elaborate protections to safeguard inventory from theft. Some businesses must worry about perishable goods and therefore spoilage control is a must. Others concern themselves about inventory age that could diminish market value. In most cases, companies have a little bit of both; inventory that spoils and inventory that becomes old.

This is where the BAR Rule comes into play. Think of inventory as bananas, apples, and raisins (BAR). Bananas spoil fast, apples spoil a little slower, and raisins last a long time before they need to be discarded.

Everybody understands this concept and can relate. Sure, the underlying spoilage time-clocks can be deployed, but if they are placed in the categories of BAR; bananas, apples or raisins; there will be a much greater acceptance of the underlying controls and a better understanding of why the controls are there in the first place. This is true for the person ordering the goods, the person receiving them, the inventory handler, and anyone else who touches the inventory in some form physically or administratively.

Everyone has eaten bananas, apples, and raisins and understands bananas brown quickly, apples rot a little later, and raisins seem to hang around for quite some time. Most inventory configurations have the same features. It makes sense, therefore, to present the challenge of managing inventory in the same way humans experience goods at home.

40

Doubting Thomas And The Law Of Disbelieving Generality

Feeling skeptical is natural. After all, there are a lot of companies and people who make outrageous claims that are hard to believe. Most individuals are not as bad as Doubting Thomas (a fictional charter that doubted everything out of proportion) but it's natural to have doubts nevertheless.

The problem with doubt though, is that it cuts both ways. There are just as many people that doubt what you say as there are people you doubt when they talk.

You can tip the scales in your favor by following the "Law of Disbelieving Generalities." Simply avoid general statements and discuss specifics, make zero claims, and let the recipient conclude your desired viewpoint based on the specific information you provide. For example, if you tell people you are a good baseball player they may doubt it: but if you tell them you played for the Pittsburgh Pirates and batted .305 they will, in all likelihood, conclude that you are superb at baseball. Note the claim of being a good baseball player was not made; however, after hearing the specifics, the recipients probably concluded that you were good nonetheless. Doubt was turned into believable credibility.

The "Law of Disbelieving Generalities" and doubt go hand and hand. You can't do much about what others say and you may doubt them, but you can control what you say and reduce their doubts about you. Don't doubt me.

41

Controls Are Like Batteries: They Discharge Gradually And Need Recharging

Business controls are processes that ensure certain approvals or justifications occur before an event proceeds. All controls should be related to protecting and improving the bottom line and established only to allow the organizational hierarchies too make decisions systematically at the appropriate levels.

By-and-large, controls are constraining to those imposed upon and comfort those who impose. It is natural to expect, therefore, that in the absence of new stimuli individuals become less disciplined. The battery is discharging.

Attacks start occurring every day in the form of "Must I fill out this form," "I don't have time to get approvals I need to do my job," or "let's skip it and see if anyone notices."

If these attacks go unchecked you will have allowed the control to discharge. A disruption must now occur in order to bring it back to its previous state.

Recharging can take many forms. For example, it can be the completion of an audit of selected processes with consequences for the violators, management discussions to reiterate the importance of controls or revisions of existing controls to ensure improved controls are followed.

Whatever form the recharging takes it must be done or the controls that took so much effort to install will fall by the wayside. Just like a battery in an automobile, if you play the radio too long while the car is not running, the battery will discharge and only bad things can happen. Indeed, if you happen to be in an isolated area, good luck trying to find help.

42

Very Few Use Buggy Whips Anymore, But Everyone Uses Computers

There was a time when buggy whips were made by the millions. Then came the horseless carriage and the world was changed. Those companies that manufactured buggy whips experienced a decline in sales every year thereafter. Even the best of the best-run companies had difficulties.

When computers were introduced, however, they took the market by storm. Those companies that manufactured computers experienced an increase in sales year after year. Even the worst of the worst-run companies succeeded.

Some would say the buggy whip manufacturers were at the wrong place at the wrong time and the computer manufacturers were at the right place at the right time. Some were lucky and some were not, right? Not really.

Looking into the future and deciding the best direction for a company to take is part of business. It is the most important decision a business can make. There can be an enormous number of mistakes in an organization, but as long as the strategic decision and corresponding direction is correct, the entity will succeed.

All businesses fall into four categories:

1. Good management practices in good markets

2. Good management practices in bad markets

3. Bad management practices in good markets

4. Bad management practices in bad markets

The highest and longest sustainable profits are created in category #1 – Good management practices in good markets. The lowest profits and usually biggest losses are experienced in category #4 – Bad management practices in bad markets.

In category #2, Good management in bad markets, the organization must have solid management practices in order to achieve profitability or losses will occur. Indeed, one good management practice that must be utilized is strategic planning so that a better business direction is determined to avoid loss of profits that will eventual occur by staying in bad markets. Just as the buggy whip manufacturers found, profits were not sustainable over the long haul.

In category #3, Bad management practices in good markets, an anomaly appears to exist. - How can a company with bad management practices succeed? That doesn't seem logical. Yet it happens all the time. Most computer manufacturers in the beginning were some of the worst run companies of all times yet they made superior profits. That's because the market was so strong that no matter how many errors were made, no matter how much inefficiency existed, and no matter how many sales opportunities were lost, there was plenty of highly profitable business to go around. Even more amazing, the profits can be sustained for quite some time as long as the market remains strong and grows faster than those who supply the market.

This brings us back to the four categories again and why it's so important to get the strategic direction correct and always compete in favorable markets; it simply boils down to improving the odds. In good markets with good management practices high profits occur and last the longest. It's the best of both worlds; but even with bad management practices high profits can still be achieved in a good market. Profits don't last as long but hopefully long enough to allow the bad management practices to be converted into good management practices and prolong profit chances.

The trick, therefore, is not to make the fatal error of remaining in a buggy whip type market that inevitably will decline and leave your business vulnerable to the effects of management mistakes. It is simply much easier when you're in good markets; errors can be made, but they don't kill you.

The last buggy whip manufacturer was properly one of the best run companies around, but they eventually closed their doors. I'll bet they used a computer to calculate their losses.

43

No One Ever Said Business Was Comfortable

Never waste time on matters that can contribute only slightly to achieving the goals you were hired to meet. As a successful business employee you must take whatever steps are necessary to ensure that you spend your time "mainly" on those areas that impact profits the most even if they are out of your comfort zone.

This is much more difficult than meets the eye. We spend far too much time in day-to-day matters that make us feel secure because of past experiences. For example, if you were once an Office Manager and spent a great deal of time managing office matters and then got promoted to CFO, the new expectations of you are to provide insightful analysis and be pro-active in the planning process, both of which typically would be out of your comfort zone. The temptation is to spend time on office problems at the expense of attending to other higher-end CFO duties that impact the bottom line the most.

Your new duties are to address the company's primary problem of poor profit planning. The CFO, therefore, must 1) be cognizant of the new set of responsibilities and avoid the temptation to attend to comfort areas such as billing, (an office manager duty), particularly if it is not a problem, and 2) be careful not to avoid the issue of poor profit planning because of the uncomfortable feelings this task elicits. The poor profit-planning problem is the highest priority area that can greatly impact the bottom line and that's where the time should be spent.

This is true in any position. All employees must rank the problems they deem most impactful on the bottom line within their own job charters and spend their time accordingly.

Resist the temptation to be in the comfort zone when it is not warranted. Be relentless. Ask yourself what is the best use of my time for the company's bottom line and act on it. Remember no one ever said business was comfortable.

44

The 1-2 Punch

McGair was a successful salesperson for a publishing company, but despite his success, he realized selling was not for him and took on a new role with a different company.

In his new position, he was responsible for collecting over 90 day past due customer accounts for the east coast region. However, unlike in his previous sales position, where was very easy to determine success based on the sales achieved, in his new role, performance measurement was a little more difficult because many of the past due accounts were disputed. The company, nevertheless, held him accountable for the over 90 day past due customer amount, but needed also to apply much judgment to assess performance because of the circumstances.

McGair started out great and won the trust of his boss. He also became well liked by almost everyone except Sonia, who was McGair's counterpart responsible for collecting over 90 day past due accounts in the west coast region. Sonia's performance could be compared directly to his performance. Sonia was not as well-liked like as McGair and she became quite jealous to the point where she started unfairly criticizing McGair in front of others including his boss. Sonia would say out loud "McGair, look at that $5,000 receivable of yours that is over 150 days past due. What is going on in your collection area?" Sonia was attacking McGair, using "DIC" Fact techniques, an acronym for Distorted Image Conveyance of Facts. Sonia stated a fact, there was a $5,000 past due account over 150 days old, but by then asking "what is going on in your collection areas?" Sonia was deviously generating doubt that McGair was not performing overall. She was stating a fact, but by also asking what is going on, conveying a distorted image that was not true. McGair had excellent collection results overall. Yet listening to Sonia assert one specific negative fact and finish with a question about the overall, she was purposely extrapolating the fact to mislead the totality, with the malicious intent of painting a harmful picture that diminished McGair.

McGair was taken back because he was not accustomed to attacks using DIC Fact techniques and never received these kinds of attacks when he was a salesperson. He didn't know what to do. Fortunately, McGair had a good friend at work that already experienced Sonia's evil ways and could help him.

McGair learned quickly from his friend and was prepared for any future attacks. When Sonia tried it again, he was ready and immediately fired back with a 1-2 punch. The first punch was to set the record straight. "Sonia, yes it is true that one account is over 150 days past due, however, collections overall are excellent." The second punch was to highlight to the same people Sonia was addressing, how misleading Sonia is by implying that because one account was not collected, the entire area was questionable. McGair would say to her "Sonia, you highlighted one particular past due item as a problem and then by immediately saying what is going on in my area, made people wonder about all items in general. You know collections are good, so why are you trying to convey a distorted image of what you know is not true?"

McGair became a fighter and spotted anytime someone tried to use DIC Fact techniques on him again. I believe it is safe to say McGair gave Sonia the 1-2 punch and knocked her clear down to the canvas. Sonia did not want a re-match.

45

When A Bear Is About To Attack

It's Ready, Fire, Aim

"**R**eady, aim, fire" is a phrase that describes planning your goals, making sure the plan is pointed in the right direction, and starting.

On occasion, however, it's better to switch the sequence because too much planning can be counterproductive. Sometimes it should be "ready, fire, aim" instead of the conventional "ready, aim, fire."

For example, Bruce plans to go to Chicago from New York City by car and on the way needs to pick up 4 packages at 4 different locations. Time is of the essence to solidify a business deal so Bruce knows he must get there very fast. Bruce also knows he must go west starting out on I-80. Hence, he immediately starts his journey, doesn't waste time planning out every detail of the trip and hits I-80 right away. Sure, he mapped out the interstate highways to follow, but he knew he could save a lot of time by just starting the journey on the first highway and only then planning every left and right turn needed to pick up the packages while driving.

As another example, if a construction company builds a series of college dorms, the project manager will plan the construction in detail, but not plan the sidewalk placement between dorms. That's because no matter how much planning takes place it is difficult to know exactly where the students will walk. Construction is started anyway and after the students move in and create path patterns, the sidewalks are installed wherever paths were made.

Of course "ready, aim, fire" makes sense the majority of the time, otherwise, not taking aim may mean accidently shooting yourself in the foot; but sometimes when a bear is about to attack, it is better to just start shooting. Fire first and aim later, who knows, the sound may scare the bear away.

46

Business Plate Spinning 101

The old entertainment act of spinning plates on top of sticks is not only difficult but also amazing. If a plate stops spinning it falls and breaks. Add a new plate to a new stick and you must go back to the first plate to speed it up again. The more plates you have, the more you must dash from plate to plate to plate to keep them all spinning. At some point you can only keep so many plates spinning at one time. If you keep adding a new plate an existing plate will fall and crash and it becomes apparent that it makes no sense to continue adding because every time a plate is added one breaks.

In business, day to day tasks are just like plates except keeping them spinning is much more difficult. That's because when you add a task you must also assess if the new task is more important than the task that will fall by the wayside.

You must know not only how many tasks are currently underway and simultaneously spinning; you must also understand the importance of each task in order to achieve the overall goals promised. You must constantly prioritize new endeavors with existing ones or you will end up spinning a lot of tasks that don't accomplish your objective. Failing to practice these principles means you will be given a failing grade in Business Plate Spinning 101.

47

Catch The Good

On most days, both good and bad things happen. You can count on it; it's like clockwork. Yet what do we notice? We notice the bad, of course. It is how humans are wired. For example, can you remember the last time you drove to work and hit every light green? Probably not, but I'll bet you can remember the last time you got caught up in a major traffic jam even if it was years ago. Let's face it, we tend to remember the bad and that's a problem because people need uplifting, need positive mental sets, and certainly need to feel appreciated for their good deeds.

Can this be fixed? Sure, simply notice the good from now on. That sounds pretty easy, but there is a hitch; it will last for only a couple of days. Sooner or later the human tendency to take for granted the good, and remember only the bad, will prevail. Then you're right back at the starting point.

The proper fix is much more involved. It must entail establishing processes that routinely "Catch the Good." This may mean creating recognition awards for specific good occurrences; encouraging company paid team lunches to celebrate the achievement of specific goals such as a successful inventory; establishing award programs such as perfect attendance awards, longevity recognition, safety awards and the like that celebrate the good; posting affirmation reminders in conspicuous places; or displaying huge banners that proclaim "catch the good."

The key is to make it "systematic"; some part of the process should automatically reinforce the concept. For example, create a report that shows the "Catch the Good" awards granted and review it each month by including it in an already established monthly performance meeting held each month. This way there is a guarantee that at least once each month people will be reminded to "Catch the Good."

Eventually, if you keep implementing systematic processes "Catching the Good" becomes part of the culture and happens naturally. The morale difference is astounding.

48

Liar, Liar Pants On Fire

Kimberly told lies all the time. They were little white lies designed to protect people's feelings. If asked, "What do you think of my new hair style?" she would answer "looks good" even if it didn't. If someone asked her, "how's it going?" she would reply, "fine" even if it were one of those days. These types of lies are told every day and are meant to protect feelings or just be cordial.

George, on the other hand, said things that were meant to diminish others or protect him from punishments he deserved. These lies are problematic for obvious reasons.

Spotting the dishonest George types is difficult. There are, however, clues to look for:

1. Listen for the word "never" or "I would never" when just a simple "no" will do. For example, when George was asked "did you complete the schedule late?" and the answer was, "I would never complete the schedule late," there was a good chance he was

not being truthful. George may have been over-compensating to hide the answer. He could have just said "no," which is much more appropriate.

2. Listen for the phrase "by the way," George says, this all the time. George is trying to minimize what he is about to say.

3. Listen for the word "that" just before a noun: George would say that Kimberly or that process. It may be a subconscious attempt to distance him from the highlighted noun.

4. Look for hot spots. These are mannerisms that the person's routine behavior does not usually show. George would bite his lip or move his legs rapidly when he was being untruthful. Kimberly was even-tempered all the time.

5. Test the person with a question. "Why should I believe you, George?" Ask it twice and see what happens. George's second answer to the question was normally accusatory, full of anger, and most often used character references. For example, "You can ask anyone who works here whether I am honest," George was possibly overcompensating. Kimberly, if asked the same question, would answer "because I've told the truth" or "because I don't lie."

It is important to have the ability to spot deceit. There is a good chance George does not always tell the truth and Kimberly is honest most of the time. You never really know for sure until something happens that proves it, but if Kimberly or George claim innocence in a troubling event, there is a pretty good chance the surveillance video they both didn't know existed will show George was the culprit and Kimberly was telling the truth. If grade school kids watched the video; they would say "Liar, liar, his pants are on fire."

49

Go To Your Customers And Employees

And Work Backwards

Business is actually very easy. Understand your customers, listen to your employees, and work backwards. This means if you are truly on top of your customer's desires, know how to solve their problems, and sincerely listen to suggestions and input from your employees, you can then take that information and develop programs that will be very successful.

Remember, customers care about themselves. They only seek pleasure and avoid pain. We all do that. If you can tap into the customers' brains and know what makes them tick, the product you're peddling and the service you offer would probably change for the better because it fulfills the customer's buy button.

For example, in the business of replacing kitchen countertops, many kitchen companies quickly became aware that not only did the customer want attractive granite countertops; they were also very concerned about how long the kitchen would be disrupted while under construction. The smart kitchen companies developed programs to articulate and give the customer a visual of the construction disruption and also commit to the numbers of days the kitchen would be off limits. They tapped into the customer's brains and knew the prospects wanted assurances and an understanding of the mess they would need to endure. These companies truly understood the customer and succeeded. On the other hand, kitchen companies that did not work backwards to understand the customer's desires, did not pitch this pain reducer to prospective customers and were blinded by their own preconceived notion that construction disruption did not matter. These companies fell by the wayside.

We all know that customers are crucial, but employees are equally important. They simply have great ideas and suggestions and, just like customers, also seek pleasure and avoid pain. You should, therefore, feed employees pleasure by rewarding great suggestions, by praising them for caring, but most of all by listening to every single word they say. That's because employees will tell you what's wrong with the company. Sure, not everything they say will be valid but by carefully listening and not quickly dismissing an employee because you think you know better, you will find most information is very useful.

A business has two components, Customers and Employees. Seek both, retrieve the information you need, and work backwards. The programs created with this approach will far outlive those programs created by top management only. Go to your customers and employees, and work backwards.

50

The One Hour Rule

E motions are part of human nature. We sometimes feel happy and sometimes feel sad. Our various emotions come and go throughout the day. They're part of life and unavoidable regardless of the efforts made to pretend they do not exist.

This can be challenging, because unless emotions are harnessed the consequences of actions taken while in a down mood could impact the working atmosphere and be problematic while attempting to achieve pre-planned goals.

Nicky and Allison both started their new jobs performing customer service problem-resolution services. Both were responsible for receiving calls about problems from customers and solving their dilemmas. Nicky and Allison's day-to-day activities consisted of taking information from customers over the phone and then personally tracking down the appropriate internal people to find solutions. Without help, neither Nicky nor Allison could possibly solve problems on her own. This meant diverting fellow employees' attention away from their ordinary duties in order to derive a resolution to a customer's problem. Most employees hated seeing Nicky and Allison because that meant a problem had to be solved and their routine duties would be disrupted. Tense emotions were inevitable and cool heads were critical.

Nicky and Allison were very good at their jobs right from the start. As time went by, however, only Allison could get results. Nicky, who at one time was considered an A player, became ineffective, hated her job, lost her once-praised abilities, and resigned.

Her boss John wondered "what happened? Why did Allison prevail and Nicky give up and what did Allison do differently than Nicky?" John, therefore, asked Allison directly and she responded, "I used the One Hour Rule and Nicky did not. It is as simple as that."

Allison explained, "I understood that my job meant confronting people to get things done. I knew it was very easy for tempers to heat up and emotional outbursts to occur. That's why whenever emotions got the best of anyone, I made a point to re-contact the confronted party within one hour and talk about anything but problems; to act like nothing emotional happened, reassuring the other person involved that I was not upset, that it was nothing personal and was just part of my job." John interrupted, "Your actions must have had a calming effect and put everything in perspective." Allison responded, "absolutely, and your probably wondering why didn't Nicky do the same? Well, Nicky took conflict personally and remained unsettled after a confrontation. She went into a funk, and didn't care how she or the confronted party felt. Nicky became bitter, but more importantly the confronted party was allowed to remain resentful and the construction of a wall between her and the confronted party was started. After a few months, there were multiple walls with many people and each wall grew taller and thicker to the point that Nicky avoided the very people with whom she needed to interact to resolve problems presented by customers. Nicky became ineffective."

John now understood, Allison succeeded because she did not allow walls to build. Nicky failed because she did the opposite and as a result had to work in a maze of walls she helped construct. Allison knew that unless positive interaction was taken within one hour, the construction of walls would start. She understood the "One Hour Rule." Nicky did not. Nicky did, however, become great at the "I have nothing but time rule" because she lost her job.

51

Get Those Monkeys Off Your Back

One of the problems for overly cooperative people is that they frequently attract monkeys who want to ride on their backs. That would be fine, but Monkeys are very distracting, make a lot of noises, and the weight of too many can be exhausting to carry around.

Well, I don't mean real monkeys, but an analogy for the countless times "unwanted tasks" somehow end up on your to-do list. It happens often and most of the time you don't realize what just hit you. It is the transfer of an unwanted assignment from one person to another in a very subtle manner.

Keep in mind; I am not talking about commitments that involve your job responsibilities. Those assignments should be completed with a smile. I do mean, however, undertakings in which you have no business being involved. They are usually thankless jobs that nobody wants and they only distract from getting your own job completed. Yet, somehow you agreed to complete the task.

People who pass monkeys to your back are very skilled at the game. They contend they can't give a task proper attention and then play to your sense of fair play, hinting that maybe you can help. They always remain silent while in a meeting when it's time for someone to volunteer for an unwanted assignment. They will act as if they are swamped and can't possibly help under the circumstances.

It is important to spot these actions. Otherwise, you are like a deer caught in the headlights. Be very careful around monkey passers as they seek out the clueless types. Also do not succumb to the silence that occurs during a meeting when it's time for someone to volunteer.

Most importantly, visualize the monkey jumping from the monkey passers back to your back. It should upset you so much that you put up your shield and defend your turf. Hey, monkeys love backs. They clung to their mother's back the day after they were born. But you're not a monkey mother; so don't act like one.

52

Hire Las Vegas Style

There is much literature devoted to hiring people. That's because it's hard to find good people to hire. Needless to say, reading the many articles and books published on how to interview effectively may be beneficial, but determining who to interview in the first place is far more critical.

That's where Las Vegas comes into play. In any gambling casino, success is a matter of probability and outcome. Casinos simply make sure the odds are in their favor. That's how they succeed.

Choosing which candidates to interview is similar. The odds must be in your favor to succeed over the long run. It simply does not matter how good an interviewer you are if you choose to interview five bad candidates in the first place. Select any one of the five candidates for the job and you end up with an ineffective, and possibly troublesome, employee.

The trick, therefore, is to improve the odds in your favor. Think like a casino. Follow these simple principles:

1. If you are advertising in mass media, for example, newspapers and internet job services, and you receive many resumes; reject any resumes that reveal too many jobs in too short a time frame, even if they have the exact experience required for a job. Sure, there may be valid reasons for holding many jobs, but the odds are the person is either negative or can't keep a job. Stick to the odds.

2. Do not choose any resume that is not presentable or has many spelling errors. Resumes of this nature may mean the person has low standards that might carry over into a job. Again, stick with the odds.

3. Eliminate resumes that applied to a different, but similar, job situation advertised many months before. The odds are they are not good at selling themselves or they would have found a job by now. If they can't sell themselves, they will also have difficulty on the job. Go with the odds. You may be passing up a great candidate who was seeking a job a couple months ago, stopped for a short period, and then started seeking employment again, but probably not.

4. Always interview out-of-state candidates who are moving into the area. They may have had a compelling reason to move that has little to do with their job. The probabilities are higher that they may be stable, competent employees.

5. If you obtain candidates through an agency that receives compensation for successfully providing a chosen job seeker, observe the parameters detailed above to increase the odds. Additionally, always pay full price. Do not negotiate a discount. The placement service person may hold the best candidates for those companies that pay full price. The premium increases your odds and is worth it.

6. Don't let headhunter organizations flood you with resumes. You could have done that on your own. Ask the placement service to forward only their top three or four candidates.

7. If you trust the individual from an actual search company and can afford the fee, discuss expectations and give feedback as you interview.

8. Insist that the selection of candidates for interviewing be performed by people one level higher on the organization chart than the candidate's direct supervisor. This will alleviate the tendency of immediate supervisors' not to select qualified candidates that could be threats to their jobs.

9. Improve your odds by encouraging referrals from employees. If there is not already a system of paying employees for referrals, then encourage the establishment of such a system. Employees are not going to refer problem people since it will reflect poorly on them. Be careful, however, they are not relatives or best friends.

10. Seek referrals from friends or organizations to which employees belong. Again the odds are improved for the same reason employee referrals are often productive.

11. Use social media like LinkedIn where experience parameters can be used for searching candidates. It may be more difficult to recruit, but it raises the odds of hiring a good employee.

All of the items above have one thing in common: they increase the chances of landing a good employee. If the Las Vegas casino principles of keeping the odds in your favor are deployed, there is a better opportunity to land capable employees. If you do otherwise, you're leaving it up to chance. You may get lucky and hit the jackpot, but probably not.

53

Promotions Go To The Less Humble

Stacy and Nick started their jobs on the same day and had the same market research responsibilities. As the years went by, both proved to be very personable people who worked hard and achieved results. It appeared they were capable of progressing into higher-level positions they coveted. Their boss, Paul, gave each excellent performance reviews over the years and considered them the top performers in his department.

Due to changes in his department, Paul had a promotion opportunity to offer. He knew he had two capable employees (Stacy and Nick) who could be promoted, but chose Stacy rather quickly. Nick was devastated and could not understand why Stacy was selected instead of him and why it occurred so rapidly. Therefore, he went to his trusted friend Beth, who had already been promoted multiple times, for help in understanding why he was not promoted. Beth was more than willing to help, but first needed to understand how both Stacy and Nick communicated with their boss.

When she understood, she gave Nick the bad news. She explained "promotions are based on three requirements and unfortunately you met only two. Stacy had all three." Beth further elaborated that both Nick and Stacy met the first and second promotion conditions: that is, 1) they both performed their job responsibilities very well, and 2) they both showed capabilities to perform at the next higher-level position. Nick, however, did not complete the third requirement. He failed to convey to his boss (Paul) that he wanted and desired very much to be promoted. Stacy, on the other hand, frequently communicated to Paul her desire to take on higher-level roles. Paul absolutely knew Stacy wanted a promotion but wasn't 100% certain that Nick felt the same way. More importantly, Paul felt pressured to select Stacy as they had had various conversations over the past three years about progressing. If Paul had selected Nick over Stacy, Paul felt Stacy would have been disappointed a lot more than Nick. Paul was conditioned by Stacy through her periodic discussions. Nick, on the other hand, not wanting to tout his own merits, stayed silent.

Nick failed to understand the fundamental principle that promotions only come to those who express their desire to be promoted. Nick did not comprehend that modesty is not a trait that is particularly good in the business world if a promotion is sought. Nick didn't get promoted, as promotions go to only the less humble.

54

The Intimidating Lead Dog

Did you ever notice how dogs interact when they are together? Put four dogs in any room and one dog always comes out as the lead dog. Keep watching and you'll notice a second in command emerges then a third and finally a fourth. There is an absolute pecking order of domination. The amazing part of this process is once the battle is settled all the dogs are OK with the order that ensues.

In the business world, it is a little different. The organizational hierarchy dictate's who is subordinate. We are not dogs and there are better ways to settle domination, but beware that is only true most of the time. Once in awhile, someone will ignore the hierarchy and try to become the dominating lead dog no matter where they are listed on the organization chart. These people learned at an early age to be somewhat of a bully and that intimidation usually gets you what you want. After all no one presented an organization chart to a 7-year-old.

Having an established lead dog isn't a bad thing as long as the lead dog is respectful once the battle is complete. Watch out, however, when you run into intimidating bully style lead dogs whose methods are to intimidate everyone including their own bosses: you may be headed into troubled waters.

Of course, spotting attempts to become a lead dog can be difficult. Watch for signs: do they ask offensive open-ended questions, become emotional and blow things out of proportion, put you on the defensive, or make you feel that you did something wrong to them? If so you may be dealing with a lead dog wanna-be.

For example, Tom the foreman on a production line in a manufacturing plant is having a problem completing requested paperwork at the end of each run. His boss Janice approaches Tom to discuss the situation and Tom immediately goes into an intimidation mode.

Tom vehemently complains that he doesn't have time for such bureaucratic nonsense because he has a production line to run. Tom further becomes emotional and tells Janice in no uncertain terms that he is tired of getting slapped around. Janice is taken back by his outburst and immediately consoles Tom and tries to make him feel better. Janice tells Tom not to worry, that from now on she will complete Part B of the form and will lobby her boss to reduce the paperwork.

Janice feels a little better and Tom was elated. Janice rationalizes that taking on her new additional duty of completing Part B of the form was necessary in order to maintain the departmental harmony. However, in retrospect, it did just the opposite. Tom became the lead dog. Janice was intimidated and didn't see what hit her. Naturally, when Janice realized what had happened, she was upset with Tom. Tensions heightened and future conflicts loomed.

Janice should have simply said to Tom that the paperwork was part of his job, and calmly asked Tom if he shows so much emotion on purpose to make others feel uneasy and, therefore, get his way.

If Janice had tactfully but deliberately confronted Tom, the battle would have ended with Tom holding the second position to Janice, who was the rightful lead dog by human organizational standards.

Now here is the amazing part: Tom would have taken the second position and been OK with it, just like in a dog's world. As second chair, Tom could have willingly accepted whatever Janice requested henceforth. Janice is, after all, not only the lead dog according to the organization hierarchy, but also the lead dog in the dog world in which Tom relates.

The key point; spot lead dog wannabes so there is never a need to relinquish the organizational lead dog status bestowed upon you. If you do otherwise you may find yourself in second position on a dog sled team where the view is not so good.

55

Win Every Battle Or Lose The War

Did you ever hear the saying, "You can win the battle, but lose the war"? Well, in business that is just not true. The business battle cry is "Win every battle or lose the war." That's right: every battle in every meeting, with every e-mail, in every face-to-face situation, but wait, in business you get to choose your battles.

Case in point, Kathy and Rebecca had similar jobs which consisted of ensuring that expenditures submitted for payment were processed per policy. This included collecting appropriate proof that services were completed in an acceptable manner, that additional charges were substantiated, and that the cost of the services and payment terms were in accordance with the contract previously agreed upon.

Kathy and Rebecca performed their jobs well and were happy to contribute. As time went by, however, Kathy became disgruntled and resigned. When Kathy had her exit interview, she explained, "no one took me seriously,

I hated needlessly chasing people for approvals, and my boss would not fight for me." Kathy said, "I just couldn't take it anymore."

Rebecca, on the other hand, had none of these frustrating feelings, despite having the exact same challenges in her job. Kathy thought this was amazing and couldn't understand how she did it. "Well, it's my last day with the company, why don't I just ask her?" Kathy thought to herself. She approached Rebecca and simply inquired, "how do you manage to keep your sanity while performing your job?"

Rebecca liked Kathy and was more than willing to help her because she knew Kathy would likely have difficulties in her next job. Rebecca, therefore, explained to her that she followed the "Win every battle or lose the war" principle. She elaborated further, "Kathy, you choose to chase every infraction and go into many battles, with the goal of winning half; I choose to go to battle only on those infractions deemed critical with the goal of winning them all." Rebecca further clarified, "once I decided to enter a battle I won every confrontation by simply being persistent. Associates knew I would be persistent and hence complied not only with the items on which I confronted, but more importantly, also on the areas not confronted. Kathy, my associates were not sure if I would confront them or not and hence it was easier for them just to comply. Once I started a battle, I was compelled to see it through no matter what. I followed the principle 'Win every battle or lose the war' and that sent a message."

Kathy went on to her next job and started practicing Rebecca's advice. It was an adjustment, but she persevered and was very successful. One year later, she bought Rebecca lunch and thanked her. Rebecca wanted to pick up the check, but Kathy insisted she would pay. Kathy asked "didn't you teach me to pick my battles and win everyone? Well, I'm paying for lunch, period." Rebecca laughed and said to Kathy "welcome to the club."

56

The Twilight Zone Upside Down

Organization

In an episode of the old TV show "The Twilight Zone," a little boy around 6 years old had magical powers. He could make it snow at will, turn an adult into a turtle, create a pony out of thin air, make people lose their ability to speak, or do anything he desired. He had absolute power and if he got mad, watch out, no one knew what he would do next. He was feared by everyone, even his parents. Every day was a challenge for his parents, and out of fear they treated their own child with kid gloves. If the child wanted pizza for breakfast, he got pizza. If he wanted two ponies that could keep him company in his bedroom, the parents would not complain. Whatever he wanted he got without a peep of protest. After all, the alternative for his parents was that they could be turned into dogs.

Of course, "The Twilight Zone" was science fiction, but nevertheless, it highlights the upside-down concept. The little boy should have been subservient to his parents, but instead, the little boy was the boss. It was upside down.

In business, the same thing can happen. Maybe not a boy with magical powers, but a management team that is so determined to appease all employees, to be friends with everyone, to make each and every person happy, that it essentially finds itself in the position of the parents from "Twilight Zone."

The signs are unmistakable. For example, employees come in late or take long lunches and no one addresses the problem; an employee decides to go above his or her bosses head to discuss problems about his or her own boss; an unjustifiable request is made but granted, none-theless, to change a procedure to make work easier for the complainer; or e-mails are sent from lower levels to higher-level people complaining about how a situation was handled, although, action was conducted properly and in the best interest of the company, management condemns the action for fear of upsetting the complainer. These are just a few examples; there are many more.

An upside-down organization creates fear of confronting the complainer, fear to implement procedural changes that may not sit well with employees, and fear to deal on a face-to-face basis. The situation is similar to that of the parents in "The Twilight Zone." Every day is surrounded by fear. Ironically, companies that try to become recognized as "the best place to work" many times become upside-down organizations. These organizations often lose their best employees because their bosses, who are trying to appease everyone, unintentionally let underlings undermine them. The boss rationalizes that allowing this to happen, serves to maintain harmony.

A business is not a democracy. A business should be operating with a clear top to bottom organizational structure. An upside-down organization is just the opposite and results in wasted energy that preserves the status quo of a tranquil atmosphere at the expense of company success. It is akin to the 6-year-old and his parents in "The Twilight Zone.' episode. It is upside down.

57

Even A Rat Seeks Success

Lily Tomlin once said, "The problem with the rat race is that even if you succeed, you're still a rat." Well, that's one way to view life and the quest for success, but there are many more. Indeed, ask five people what they consider "success" and you will probably get five different answers.

Success is in the eye of the beholder. Some will tell you it's the journey. Some will say it's when you have amassed a large amount of money. Others will insist achieving happiness is all that matters. They are all correct. In fact, success is one of the most written-about topics of all time. Here are just a few comments that have been made regarding success.

- "A successful man is the one who finds out what is the matter with his business before his competitors do." (Ray L Smith)

- "A successful man is one who can lay a firm foundation with the bricks others have thrown at him." (David Brinkley)

- "Success is going from failure to failure without loss of enthusiasm." (Winston Churchill)

- "Success is relative. It is what we can make of the mess we have made of things." (T. S. Eliot)

- "You never become a howling success by just howling." (Bob Harrington)

- "Success means only doing what you do well, letting someone else do the rest." (Goldstein S. Truism)

- "Success is a matter of luck. Ask any failure." (Earl Wilson)

As you can see, everyone thinks of success differently. Sure, we may all be rats in a rat race, but so what? Even rats search for the best cheese. Shouldn't that be considered success even for a rat?

58

Fruit Will Not Grow Without Its Core

A company has a soul. It is defined by the core values it follows and the culture that results from the day- to-day practice of its core values.

Core values are the principles that top management believes in and wants everyone to follow. They may consist of integrity, respect, customer satisfaction, appreciation, recognition, understanding the competition, or many others. They are the attributes that a top management team would like all employees to practice each and every day.

Core values are critical for success and, therefore, should be published for all to see. All employees should not only understand the values posted, but live by them. If an employee refuses, he or she may be a bad fit and may not belong in the organization. That employee, after all, does not share the same values.

One of the biggest challenges with a core values statement is that many times it lays dormant. It can become a fixture on the wall that no one notices. It can be ridiculed or touted as corny. The risk of mockery is real and may be warranted if the core values are not applied. Therefore, to minimize the risk of core value apathy, mechanisms should be implemented to ensure that each core value is practiced. That may mean giving an appreciation award, or special recognition ceremony that encourages practicing core values. It could be a statement explaining each core value that is discussed during a routine meeting, or a system that collects the number of times a core value was followed.

The point is, in order for core values to become part of the company's culture, there must be procedures, systems, and reward structures to incorporate the values into practical applications. Failure to do so may result in a fruit without a core. It will not develop.

59

Sell Like A Doctor

Would you characterize a doctor as a salesperson? Probably not, yet doctors sell almost every day. Oh, it may not seem like selling, but each time a doctor sees a patient, he or she is advocating a remedy to a health problem. Most doctors don't see themselves as sales-people but whether they realize it or not, they are performing a sales task and they are very good at it. Dr. Vay, for example, would go to great pains to explain to her patient a health issue discovered and the steps needed to correct the problem. That was selling. She believed that telling a patient just to take their medicine without an explanation would be crazy.

Naturally, Dr. Vay's closing ratio was 99%, meaning only 1% refused to accept what she said and went to another doctor. That sounds unusual, but not really. Most doctors hit closing ratios in the 90 percent range.

The question then becomes, why is the ratio so high? In most other businesses, the numbers are not normally that high.

Why do doctors' patients (customers) say yes so quickly, yet customers of business products say no much more often than they say yes? What is the missing ingredient?

The answer is simple. Business salespeople tend to push a product or service based on their perceptions of what it can do for the customer. A company salesperson, unlike the doctor, spends very little time determining the customers' problems that need to be satisfied by the product or service for sale. The business salesperson spends very little time diagnosing, while Dr. Vay and most other doctors do the opposite; they spend the majority of their time diagnosing. To Dr. Vay and all the other doctors it would be malpractice not to operate in this way. The patients understand what doctors are doing and are comforted by the diagnosis. The patient quite naturally accepts the remedy. Closing the sale is easy for Dr. Vay and her associates.

That begs the question: Why do most business salespeople spend so little time asking questions to find out what makes the potential customer tick? Why don't they copy a doctor's approach and spend a lot of their time on diagnosis, then determine how their product or service will help?

I really don't know, maybe its ego or maybe its stupidity, but business salespeople would benefit greatly from acting like doctors and performing diagnoses accordingly. Sure, they are not doctors, but it doesn't matter. What matters is the comfort customers feel when their specific situation is understood. Closing ratios will certainly increase. They may not rise to 99% like Dr. Vay's, but they will certainly be higher than those attained without a diagnosis.

60

Don't Waste Time And Energy
Teaching A Pig To Sing

George Bernard Shaw once said "Never try to teach a pig to sing. It wastes your time and it annoys the pig." What Shaw was highlighting applies to business. Simply don't waste time and energy teaching people who do not want to learn, especially if they show any signs of being annoyed.

We all know that time is precious. It stands to reason that spending even one minute of time on ungrateful participants who don't realize how fortunate they are to be taught, should simply not happen.

There is no return for the company, no return for you, and no return for the pig.

61

Embrace The Control Concept

Or Be Square

Controls are any device, system, authorization process, established procedure, or other mechanisms that establish order and accountability to minimize the chance of unintended consequences and maximize results. It recognizes that people have different experiences and expertise and can make judgment errors and that some decisions should be made at higher levels. It also recognizes that people are not perfect in their moral compass and can be compromised particularly when temptation is present or a conflict of interest exists.

Problems resulting from control ineffectiveness can be reduced by funneling decisions through proper channels to more knowledgeable people and or to people at higher organizational levels where the individual generally has more experience and more likely to make the correct decision. Problems can also be minimized by reducing the temptation and conflict of interest present in the decision.

The control concept is either embraced or opposed. Those that fight controls, delay implementation of controls, or excessively condemn controls, are people who usually do not understand basic management principles or the concept of cost-benefit and are less capable of managing larger organizations. They are more likely than others to participate in questionable transactions or hide theft. They lack guts to confront a condition or situation and feel comfortable with an ineffective status quo. They also put their own day to day comfort over the best interests of the company and their uncooperative behavior may represent an attempt to escape the consequences of poor performance. More importantly they impede and confuse those that do understand why controls are necessary.

You can always tell who are anti controls by their statements made. They will say; you don't trust me or I don't have time. They may ask; what do you want me to do, my job or the paperwork? You may hear; I'll get to it if I have time and when I'm done with my real job. The bottom line is there is no place for anti-control people in an organization. They cannot be relied upon to implement or enforce controls and likely will sabotage the effectiveness of controls through either overt action or complacent inaction.

62

Ed Beat Jean But She Got The Last Laugh

Ed was the department head for the east coast customer service department and Jean was the department head for the west. Ed & Jean were married and started at the same time.

The employees in each department did the exact same work, had the exact same challenges, received similar compensation, and were the same for all practical purposes. The departments existed side by side in the same office building and members of each department intermixed quite often during lunch and elsewhere.

Ed's style was one of encouraging laughter. He razzed people, kidded around with them and when he heard laughter Ed was happy. Jean, on the other hand, was a strict disciplined supervisor. She believed if laughter occurred, employees were probably loafing and robbing time from the company. Jean rationalized that only continual nonstop business would result in maximum productivity.

At the end of each quarter, the accounting department would publish customer service productivity stats and the Human Resources department would score morale based on surveys taken.

Ed & Jean couldn't wait for the results to be published and often would wager bets.

At first, Jean kept winning using her keep your nose to the grindstone style, but as time went by Ed with his encouraging laughter approach started to beat Jean routinely and won the last three quarter contests.

When the most recent quarter results came out, Ed won again. This upset Jean, especially since she believed she probably would be teased by Ed at dinner later that day. Jean now lost four times in a row and had to ask why, and as much as she hated, thought it best to ask Ed what magic he was using.

When asked, Ed promptly explained "I encouraged laughter. "I also believe that laughter takes away any fear in the atmosphere and when people feel they can speak out, better ideas flow. People work smarter not harder." Ed further elaborated, "that doesn't happen right away. That's why I initially lost, but eventually the ideas develop and productivity improved."

Ed also said "people like to razz others and kid around which makes it enjoyable to come to work, but under a strict atmosphere, employees will report off a lot more and there is certainly higher turnover.

Ed was about to go on further to explain his laughter theory, but realized that he was enlightening his wife Jean on how to win the future contests. Jean started laughing and told Ed "I like your laughter theory, I think I'll try it." Jean did just that and eventually won just as many as she lost. Jean got the last laugh after-all.

63

It Was A Shut Out

Frank, the supervisor at James Bond Enterprises, was a reasonable man and took pride in how he treated equally the people that worked for him directly. That was until one day when he did some soul searching and concluded he favored one direct report (Ethan) over another direct report (Lenore). This upset Frank because he did not want to give anyone special treatment. Frank, therefore, decided that if he logged every interaction he had with Ethan and Lenore over the next 5 days, it might help him determine if there was anything he could do to fix it.

On the first day, Frank requested that Ethan and Lenore complete an assignment by Wednesday. Lenore immediately said, "It's not possible to complete that by Wednesday," while Ethan said "Wednesday is difficult, but I can definitely complete it by Friday." Frank quickly realized that Lenore took a defeatist approach that made him feel troubled, while Ethan, on the other hand, by being realistic yet positive gave Frank comfort. Frank learned one of the reasons he felt discomfort with Lenore and favored Ethan.

On the second day, it happened to be that time of year when performance reviews and raises were normally completed. However, because of a glitch in the computer system it was delayed for one week. Frank informed both Ethan and Lenore of the problem. Lenore told Frank, she wasn't happy, needed a raise, and couldn't wait a week even though she understood the raise would be retroactive. Lenore further explained to Frank that she and her husband had many bills to pay and needed to catch up. Ethan also took the opportunity to discuss his raise. He described to Frank how he believed he deserved a raise because of his accomplishments over the past year. Frank reflected on how he felt with both conversations and concluded that Lenore's comments made him feel uneasy because he did not believe it was appropriate to justify a raise based on need. Frank also thought it wasn't his responsibility to concern himself with Lenore's personal finances. On the other hand, Ethan made Frank feel good by highlighting his accomplishments.

On the third day, Frank introduced a new method of processing paperwork. Lenore said, "what's wrong with the current method?" and Ethan said "that's great, what are the benefits?" Frank logged that event as bad feelings with Lenore and good feelings with Ethan.

On the fourth day, Lenore said to Frank, "don't expect much from me today. I partied too hard last night." Although Frank knew that Ethan had taken part in the same festivities, Ethan said nothing. Frank logged that event as unfavorable for Lenore and favorable for Ethan.

On the fifth day, Frank talked to Lenore and Ethan together. Frank asked both to work on a team with Andrew; Andrew was arguably the most difficult person in the company. Lenore immediately said, "I can't stand working with Andrew" while Ethan said, "I'll do my best." Frank recorded that event as a bad feeling with Lenore and a good feeling with Ethan.

At the end of the fifth day, the score was five for Ethan and zero for Lenore. It was a shutout; not even close. Frank realized he was justified in feeling the way he did. He wasn't discriminating against Lenore; he was favoring actions that were more appropriate by Ethan. Frank no longer felt guilty and realized that he didn't need to change, Lenore did.

64

The 5 Laws Of Interviewing

Sometimes a company or organization has too many problems to overcome and it is time for you to move on. Not a good thought, but a reality. That's why it is always good to be prepared to switch to a new organization when that time comes.

Of course, you will need to develop a resume that is concise, meaningful, and adequate enough to land an interview. Once that occurs, the real challenge arises: winning the job, especially because you're probably not prepared to sell yourself (unless you are a salesperson). There is hope, however, because interviewing can be addressed logically.

There are five essential principles that should be followed. I call them the "5 Laws of Interviewing."

1. <u>Law of Protocol</u> – There are two types of protocols: 1) items that need little explanation, such as looking a person in the eye, shaking hands firmly,

not slouching, and sending a follow-up thank-you letter, and 2) items that need elaboration, such as greeting the interviewer in a non-timid manner and wearing proper attire. Both types are important and both are a challenge. Greeting the interviewer should not be tentative. You should powerfully say, "glad to meet you." Ask, "how's your day going?" The greeting, along with your attire is your first impression. This must go flawlessly. Regarding proper attire, if the company is a construction company and business casual is the norm; if you are a man wear a sport coat but not a tie. Do wear a suit if the company is the type where ties are worn every day, even if the tie is worn with a sport coat. For woman, wear a non-revealing business suit, and if that is too much, a non-revealing alternative. Women should never wear attire that accentuates or shows off their bodies. Oh, it may work, but the job may be offered for the wrong reasons, and that will be trouble later.

2. <u>Law of Association</u> – Everyone has experienced events in their lives the mere remembrance gives them pleasure. It could be an event with their kids, or it could be a favorite football team winning a critical game. There are an endless number of examples, but the critical point is that everybody has them. If you can discover these areas quickly about the interviewer and discuss early in the interview, you have made the interviewer feel good by reminiscing. When this occurs, he or she will associate the good feelings with you. Sure, it may be difficult to recognize the triggers, but check the

surroundings for clues. There may be a picture hanging, or an object close by, that gives you a hint. Also, before the interview, search the internet and ask others that may know. An important aspect of creating a positive association is to generate associated feelings very quickly early in the interview. This will position the interviewer to feel good in your presence and want you to be the one chosen. It may also allow the interviewer to overlook possible areas of concern that come up later.

3. <u>Law of Self-Imposed Criteria</u> – Very early during the interview process, it is imperative to understand the "buy button" that's in the interviewer's head. Ask, "what are you looking for?" or inquire "what kinds of personality traits are necessary?" Keep in mind that the vast majority of interviewers will be judging you based on their own life experiences. Hence, ask the interviewer, "what qualities do you believe are needed to be successful on this job?" or ask, "you've been with the company for some time, how have you succeeded?"

4. <u>Law of Disbelieving Generalities</u> – After you developed associated good feelings and determined the "buy buttons" of the interviewer using the appropriate protocol expected, you are then in a much better position to answer questions that arise. The trick to answering the questions is to reply to each one in a very precise manner. Avoid generalities. This means provide a statement that is factual, but does not provide a conclusion. Position your statement such that the interviewer concludes

you are superior at a skill based on the detail you presented. Avoid statements that directly tell the interviewer you have excellent skills in a certain area. The interviewer may or may not believe you. It is much more powerful when the interviewer concludes you have excellent skills rather than telling them you do. For example, if someone asks about your supervisory skills, and you say, "I am good at supervising people," he or she may or may not believe you. However, if you say, "I have supervised many people in the past and no one quit," the interviewer will no doubt conclude you are good at supervision. Note you never said you had good supervisory skills, the interviewer concluded that based on the detail offered.

5. <u>Law of Negative Hypotheses</u> – The final law to recognize is that most people get hired not because they have excellent interpersonal and other job-related skills, but instead because they have all the skills needed and the interviewer had the least number of doubts compared to other candidates. I call them negative hypotheses. They are beliefs not based on facts, but instead based on feelings that developed due to past experiences. During the interview, you may sense that the interviewer has apprehension about a skill set you have. That's a negative hypothesis and you will not get the job unless you convince the interviewer that his or her negative hypothesis is not true. That can only happen through discussing specifics, but not making general self-promoting positive claims. It is imperative to end the interview without any negative

hypotheses. That's a challenge because you never really know. Hence, ask, "Is there anything in my background that would preclude you from considering me a serious candidate?" That should flush out any negative hypotheses and you can proceed to erase them by discussing specifics in an inconclusive manner.

To master the above, you will need feedback on how well you followed the 5 Laws of Interviewing. It is imperative, therefore, to grade your performance immediately after each interview. The hardest part of grading your performance will be steps 2 and 3 because there is a natural tendency to wait for interviewers to take the lead and wait for their questions. It is hard to discuss self-imposed criteria or generate associated good feelings once questions start. You will need to take charge of interviews early on, ask questions, and have conversations before interviewers start asking their own questions.

65

Life Is Give And Take, Balance It Wisely

Work is important. Make no mistake about it. However, you must not forget it is only a means to an end to achieve happiness with your family, your friends, and yourself. We spend so much time at work that we sometimes don't remember why we are there in the first place. Sure, work commands our time and of course, we should work hard, but too much of anything is usually not good. Balance is the key.

If you're performing effectively and understand how your goals tie into the goals of the company, you will know when a situation is significant enough to put in extra work hours. Under these circumstances (which should be infrequent) you may need to sacrifice attending your daughter's soccer game. The company truly needs you and you should respond. There is also nothing wrong in dedicating extra hours at work even when it is not critical, as long as it does not conflict with family matters and you don't become a workaholic, which is akin to having a disease.

The point is to have Balance; work hard during the day and manage your tasks such that they do not rob "quality" time from friends and family when they need you and you need them.

Life is give and take, balance it wisely.